Vainly walked he through the forest,
Sought for bird or beast and found none.

The Song of Hiawatha

An Epic Poem

By

Henry Wadsworth Longfellow

Contents

INTRODUCTORY NOTE.

The Song of Hiawatha first appeared in 1855. In it Mr. Longfellow has woven together the beautiful traditions of the American Indians into one grand and delightful epic poem. The melodies of its rhythm and measure flow from his classic pen in unison with the hoof-beats of the bison, the tremulous thunder of the Falls of Minnehaha, the paddle strokes of the Indian canoeist, and he has done more to immortalize in song and story the life and environments of the red man of America than any other writer, save perhaps J. Fenimore Cooper. It was from a perusal of the Finnish epic "Kalevala" that both the measure and the style of "Hiawatha" was suggested to Mr. Longfellow. In fact, it might appropriately be named the "Kalevala" of North America. Mr. Long-fellow derived his knowledge of Indian legends from Schoolcraft's Algic Researches and other books, from Heckewelder's Narratives, from Black Hawk, with his display of Sacs and Foxes on Boston Common, and from the Ojibway chief, Kahge-gagah-bowh, whom he entertained at his own home.

Hiawatha had a wide circulation, both in America and Europe, and was universally admired by readers and critics on both Continents. Large audiences gathered to hear it read by public readers. It was set to music by Stoepel, and at the Boston Theater it was rendered with ex-planatory readings by the famous elocutionist, Matilda Heron. The highest encomiums were passed upon it by such critics of ripe scholar-ship as Emerson and Hawthorne. A part of it was translated into Latin and used as an academic text book. Those who wish to read more about it will find interest and pleasure in perusing the masterly criti-cisms of Dr. O. W. Holmes in the Annals of the Massachusetts Historical Society, and that of Horatio Hale in the Proceedings of the American Association for the Advancement of Science, 1881.

INTRODUCTION.

Should you ask me, whence these stories?
Whence these legends and traditions,
With the odors of the forest,
With the dew and damp of meadows,
5   With the curling smoke of wigwams,
With the rushing of great rivers,
With their frequent repetitions,
And their wild reverberations,
As of thunder in the mountains?
10   I should answer, I should tell you,
"From the forests and the prairies,
From the great lakes of the Northland,
From the land of the Ojibways,
From the land of the Dacotahs,
15   From the mountains, moors, and fen-lands,

Where the heron, the Shuh-shuh-gah,
Feeds among the reeds and rushes.
I repeat them as I heard them
From the lips of Nawadaha,
20   The musician, the sweet singer."
        Should you ask where Nawadaha
Found these songs so wild and wayward,
Found these legends and traditions,
I should answer, I should tell you,
25   "In the bird's-nests of the forest,
In the lodges of the beaver,

In the hoof-prints of the bison,
In the eyry of the eagle!
        "All the wild-fowl sang them to him,
30   In the moorlands and the fen-lands,
In the melancholy marshes;
Chetowaik, the plover, sang them,
Mahn, the loon, the wild goose, Wawa,
The blue heron, the Shuh-shuh-gah
35   And the grouse, the Mushkodasa!"
        If still further you should ask me,
Saying, "Who was Nawadaha?
Tell us of this Nawadaha,"
I should answer your inquiries
40   Straightway in such words as follow.
        "In the Vale of Tawasentha,
In the green and silent valley,
By the pleasant water-courses,
Dwelt the singer Nawadaha.
45   Round about the Indian village

Spread the meadows and the cornfields,
And beyond them stood the forest,
Stood the groves of singing pine-trees,
Green in Summer, white in Winter,
50   Ever sighing, ever singing.
        "And the pleasant water-courses,
You could trace them through the valley,
By the rushing in the Spring-time,
By the alders in the Summer,
55   By the white fog in the Autumn,
By the black line in the Winter;
And beside them dwelt the singer,
In the vale of Tawasentha,
In the green and silent valley.
60   "There he sang of Hiawatha,
Sang the Song of Hiawatha,
Sang his wondrous birth and being,
How he prayed and how he fasted,
How he lived, and toiled, and suffered
65   That the tribes of men might prosper,
That he might advance his people!"
        Ye who love the haunts of Nature,
Love the sunshine of the meadow,
Love the shadow of the forest,
70   Love the wind among the branches,
And the rain-shower and the snow-storm,
And the rushing of great rivers
Through their palisades of pine-trees,
And the thunder in the mountains,
75   Whose innumerable echoes
Flap like eagles in their eyries;—
Listen to these wild traditions,
To this Song of Hiawatha!
        Ye who love a nation's legends
80   Love the ballads of a people,
That like voices from afar off
Call to us to pause and listen,
Speak in tones so plain and childlike,
Scarcely can the ear distinguish
85   Whether they are sung or spoken;—
Listen to this Indian Legend,

To this Song of Hiawatha!
Ye whose hearts are fresh and simple,
Who have faith in God and Nature,
90   Who believe that in all ages
Every human heart is human,
That in even savage bosoms
There are longings, yearnings, strivings
For the good they comprehend not,
95   That the feeble hands and helpless,
Groping blindly in the darkness,
Touch God's right hand in that darkness,
And are lifted up and strengthened;—
Listen to this simple story,
100   To this song of Hiawatha!
Ye who sometimes, in your rambles
Through the green lanes of the country,
Where the tangled barberry-bushes
Hang their tufts of crimson berries
105   Over stone walls gray with mosses,
Pause by some neglected graveyard,
For a while to muse, and ponder
On a half-effaced inscription,
Written with little skill of song-craft,
110   Homely phrases, but each letter
Full of hope and yet of heart-break,
Full of all the tender pathos
Of the Here and the Hereafter;—
Stay and read this rude inscription,
115   Read this song of Hiawatha!

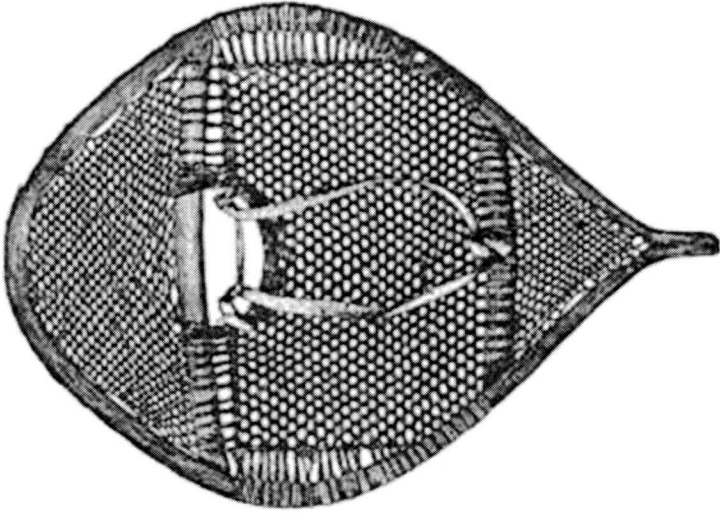

Ojibway Snow Shoe.

"Smoked the Calumet, the Peace-Pipe."

I. - THE PEACE-PIPE.

On the Mountains of the Prairie,
On the great Red Pipe-stone Quarry,
Gitche Manito, the mighty,
He the Master of Life, descending,
5 On the red crags of the quarry
Stood erect, and called the nations,
Called the tribes of men together.
From his footprints flowed a river,
Leaped into the light of morning,
10 O'er the precipice plunging downward
Gleamed like Ishkoodah, the comet.
And the Spirit, stooping earthward,
With his finger on the meadow
Traced a winding pathway for it,
15 Saying to it, "Run in this way!"
From the red stone of the quarry
With his hand he broke a fragment,
Moulded it into a pipe-head,
Shaped and fashioned it with figures;

20   From the margin of the river
Took a long reed for a pipe-stem,
With its dark green leaves upon it,
Filled the pipe with bark of willow,
With the bark of the red willow;
25   Breathed upon the neighboring forest,
Made its great boughs chafe together,
Till in flame they burst and kindled;
And erect upon the mountains,
Gitche Manito, the mighty,
30   Smoked the calumet, the Peace-Pipe,
As a signal to the nations.

And the smoke rose slowly, slowly,
Through the tranquil air of morning,
First a single line of darkness,
35   Then a denser, bluer vapor,
Then a snow-white cloud unfolding,
Like the tree-tops of the forest,
Ever rising, rising, rising,
Till it touched the top of heaven,
40   Till it broke against the heaven,
And rolled outward all around it.
From the Vale of Tawasentha,
From the Valley of Wyoming,
From the groves of Tuscaloosa,
45   From the far-off Rocky Mountains,
From the Northern lakes and rivers,
All the tribes beheld the signal,
Saw the distant smoke ascending,
The Pukwana of the Peace-Pipe.
50   And the Prophets of the nations
Said: "Behold it, the Pukwana!
By this signal from afar off,
Bending like a wand of willow,
Waving like a hand that beckons,
55   Gitche Manito, the mighty,
Calls the tribes of men together,
Calls the warriors to his council!"

Down the rivers, o'er the prairies,
Came the warriors of the nations,
60 Came the Delawares and Mohawks,
Came the Choctaws and Camanches,
Came the Shoshonies and Blackfeet,
Came the Pawnees and Omahas,
Came the Mandans and Dacotahs,
65 Came the Hurons and Ojibways,
All the warriors drawn together
By the signal of the Peace-Pipe,
To the Mountains of the Prairie,
To the great Red Pipe-stone Quarry.
70 And they stood there on the meadow,
With their weapons and their war-gear,
Painted like the leaves of Autumn,
Painted like the sky of morning,
Wildly glaring at each other;
75 In their faces stern defiance,
In their hearts the feuds of ages,
The hereditary hatred,
The ancestral thirst of vengeance.
Gitche Manito, the mighty,
80 The creator of the nations,
Looked upon them with compassion,
With paternal love and pity;
Looked upon their wrath and wrangling
But as quarrels among children,
85 But as feuds and fights of children!
Over them he stretched his right hand,
To subdue their stubborn natures,
To allay their thirst and fever,
By the shadow of his right hand;
90 Spake to them with voice majestic
As the sound of far-off waters
Falling into deep abysses,
Warning, chiding, spake in this wise:—
"O my children! my poor children!
95 Listen to the words of wisdom,
Listen to the words of warning,
From the lips of the Great Spirit,
From the Master of Life, who made you!

"I have given you lands to hunt in,
100   I have given you streams to fish in,

I have given you bear and bison,
I have given you roe and reindeer,
I have given you brant and beaver,
Filled the marshes full of wild fowl,
105   Filled the rivers full of fishes;
Why then are you not contented?
Why then will you hunt each other?
        "I am weary of your quarrels,
Weary of your wars and bloodshed,
110   Weary of your prayers for vengeance,
Of your wranglings and dissensions;
All your strength is in your union,
All your danger is in discord;
Therefore be at peace henceforward,
115   And as brothers live together.
        "I will send a Prophet to you,
A Deliverer of the nations,
Who shall guide you and shall teach you,
Who shall toil and suffer with you.
120   If you listen to his counsels,
You will multiply and prosper;
If his warnings pass unheeded,
You will fade away and perish!
        "Bathe now in the stream before you,
125   Wash the war-paint from your faces,
Wash the blood-stains from your fingers,
Bury your war-clubs and your weapons,
Break the red stone from this quarry,
Mould and make it into Peace-Pipes,

130   Take the reeds that grow beside you,
       Deck them with your brightest feathers,
       Smoke the calumet together,
       And as brothers live henceforward!"
             Then upon the ground the warriors
135   Threw their cloaks and shirts of deer-skin,
       Threw their weapons and their war-gear,
       Leaped into the rushing river,
       Washed the war-paint from their faces.
       Clear above them flowed the water,
140   Clear and limpid from the footprints
       Of the Master of Life descending;
       Dark below them flowed the water,
       Soiled and stained with streaks of crimson,
       As if blood were mingled with it!
145   From the river came the warriors,
       Clean and washed from all their war-paint;
       On the banks their clubs they buried,
       Buried all their warlike weapons,
       Gitche Manito, the mighty,
150   The Great Spirit, the creator,

Smiled upon his helpless children!
     And in silence all the warriors
Broke the red stone of the quarry,
Smoothed and formed it into Peace-Pipes,
155   Broke the long reeds by the river,
Decked them with their brightest feathers,
And departed each one homeward,
While the Master of Life, ascending,
Through the opening of cloud-curtains,
160   Through the doorways of the heaven,
Vanished from before their faces,
In the smoke that rolled around him,
The Pukwana of the Peace-Pipe!

II. - THE FOUR WINDS.

"Honor be to Mudjekeewis!"
Cried the warriors, cried the old men,
When he came in triumph homeward
With the sacred Belt of Wampum,
5 From the regions of the North-Wind,
From the kingdom of Wabasso,
From the land of the White Rabbit.
He had stolen the Belt of Wampum
From the neck of Mishe-Mokwa,
10 From the Great Bear of the mountains,
From the terror of the nations,
As he lay asleep and cumbrous
On the summit of the mountains,
Like a rock with mosses on it,
15 Spotted brown and gray with mosses.
        Silently he stole upon him,
Till the red nails of the monster
Almost touched him, almost scared him,
Till the hot breath of his nostrils
20 Warmed the hands of Mudjekeewis,
As he drew the Belt of Wampum
Over the round ears, that heard not,
Over the small eyes, that saw not,
Over the long nose and nostrils,
25 The black muffle of the nostrils,
Out of which the heavy breathing
Warmed the hands of Mudjekeewis.
        Then he swung aloft his war-club,
Shouted loud and long his war-cry,

30 Smote the mighty Mishe-Mokwa
In the middle of the forehead,
Right between the eyes he smote him.
          With the heavy blow bewildered,
Rose the Great Bear of the mountains;
35 But his knees beneath him trembled,
And he whimpered like a woman,
As he reeled and staggered forward,
As he sat upon his haunches;
And the mighty Mudjekeewis,
40 Standing fearlessly before him,
Taunted him in loud derision,
Spake disdainfully in this wise:—
          "Hark you, Bear! you are a coward,
And no Brave, as you pretended;
45 Else you would not cry and whimper
Like a miserable woman!
Bear! you know our tribes are hostile,
Long have been at war together;
Now you find that we are strongest,
50 You go sneaking in the forest,
You go hiding in the mountains!
Had you conquered me in battle
Not a groan would I have uttered;
But you, Bear! sit here and whimper,
55 And disgrace your tribe by crying,
Like a wretched Shaugodaya,
Like a cowardly old woman!"
          Then again he raised his war-club,
Smote again the Mishe-Mokwa
60 In the middle of his forehead,
Broke his skull, as ice is broken
When one goes to fish in Winter.
Thus was slain the Mishe-Mokwa,
He the Great Bear of the mountains,
65 He the terror of the nations.
          "Honor be to Mudjekeewis!"
With a shout exclaimed the people,
"Honor be to Mudjekeewis!
Henceforth he shall be the West-Wind,
70 And hereafter and forever

Shall he hold supreme dominion
Over all the winds of heaven.
Call him no more Mudjekeewis,
Call him Kabeyun, the West-Wind!"
75   Thus was Mudjekeewis chosen
Father of the Winds of Heaven.
For himself he kept the West-Wind,
Gave the others to his children;
Unto Wabun gave the East-Wind,
80   Gave the South to Shawondasee,
And the North-Wind, wild and cruel,
To the fierce Kabibonokka.
        Young and beautiful was Wabun;
He it was who brought the morning,
85   He it was whose silver arrows
Chased the dark o'er hill and valley;
He it was whose cheeks were painted
With the brightest streaks of crimson,
And whose voice awoke the village,
90   Called the deer, and called the hunter.
        Lonely in the sky was Wabun;
Though the birds sang gayly to him,
Though the wild-flowers of the meadow
Filled the air with odors for him,
95   Though the forests and the rivers
Sang and shouted at his coming,
Still his heart was sad within him,
For he was alone in heaven.
        But one morning, gazing earthward,
100 While the village still was sleeping,
And the fog lay on the river,
Like a ghost, that goes at sunrise,
He beheld a maiden walking
All alone upon a meadow,
105 Gathering water-flags and rushes
By a river in the meadow.
        Every morning, gazing earthward,
Still the first thing he beheld there
Was her blue eyes looking at him,
110 Two blue lakes among the rushes.
And he loved the lonely maiden,

14

Who thus waited for his coming;
For they both were solitary,
She on earth and he in heaven.
115   And he wooed her with caresses,
Wooed her with his smile of sunshine,
With his flattering words he wooed her,
With his sighing and his singing,
Gentlest whispers in the branches,
120 Softest music, sweetest odors,
Till he drew her to his bosom,
Folded in his robes of crimson,
Till into a star he changed her,
Trembling still upon his bosom;
125 And forever in the heavens
They are seen together walking,
Waban and the Wabun-Annung,
Wabun and the Star of Morning.
   But the fierce Kabibonokka
130 Had his dwelling among icebergs,
In the everlasting snow-drifts,
In the kingdom of Wabasso,
In the land of the White Rabbit.
He it was whose hand in Autumn
135 Painted all the trees with scarlet,
Stained the leaves with red and yellow;
He it was who sent the snow-flakes,
Sifting, hissing through the forest,
Froze the ponds, the lakes, the rivers,
140 Drove the loon and sea-gull southward,
Drove the cormorant and curlew
To their nests of sedge and sea-tang
In the realms of Shawondasee.
   Once the fierce Kabibonokka
145 Issued from his lodge of snow-drifts,
From his home among the icebergs,
And his hair, with snow besprinkled,
Streamed behind him like a river,
Like a black and wintry river,
150 As he howled and hurried southward,
Over frozen lakes and moorlands.
   There among the reeds and rushes

Found he Shingebis, the diver,
Trailing strings of fish behind him,
155   O'er the frozen fens and moorlands,
Lingering still among the moorlands,
Though his tribe had long departed
To the land of Shawondasee.
       Cried the fierce Kabibonokka,
160   "Who is this that dares to brave me?
Dares to stay in my dominions,
When the Wawa has departed,
When the wild-goose has gone southward,
And the heron, the Shuh-shuh-gah,
165   Long ago departed southward?
I will go into his wigwam,
I will put his smouldering fire out!"
       And at night Kabibonokka
To the lodge came wild and wailing,
170   Heaped the snow in drifts about it,
Shouted down into the smoke-flue,
Shook the lodge-poles in his fury,
Flapped the curtain of the door-way.
Shingebis, the diver, feared not,
175   Shingebis, the diver, cared not;
Four great logs had he for fire-wood,
One for each moon of the winter,
And for food the fishes served him.
By his blazing fire he sat there,
180   Warm and merry, eating, laughing,
Singing, "O Kabibonokka,
You are but my fellow-mortal!"
       Then Kabibonokka entered,
And though Shingebis, the diver,
185   Felt his presence by the coldness,
Felt his icy breath upon him,
Still he did not cease his singing,
Still he did not leave his laughing,
Only turned the log a little,
190   Only made the fire burn brighter,
Made the sparks fly up the smoke-flue.
       From Kabibonokka's forehead,
From his snow-besprinkled tresses,

Drops of sweat fell fast and heavy,
195 Making dints upon the ashes,

"I have given you streams to fish in."

As along the eaves of lodges,
As from drooping boughs of hemlock,
Drips the melting snow in spring-time,
Making hollows in the snow-drifts.
200   Till at last he rose defeated,
Could not bear the heat and laughter,
Could not bear the merry singing,
But rushed headlong through the door-way,
Stamped upon the crusted snow-drifts,
205 Stamped upon the lakes and rivers,
Made the snow upon them harder,
Made the ice upon them thicker,

Challenged Shingebis, the diver,
To come forth and wrestle with him,
210   To come forth and wrestle naked
On the frozen fens and moorlands.
      Forth went Shingebis, the diver,
Wrestled all night with the North-Wind,
Wrestled naked on the moorlands
215   With the fierce Kabibonokka,
Till his panting breath grew fainter,
Till his frozen grasp grew feebler,
Till he reeled and staggered backward,
And retreated, baffled, beaten,
220   To the kingdom of Wabasso,
To the land of the White Rabbit,
Hearing still the gusty laughter,
Hearing Shingebis, the diver,
Singing, "O Kabibonokka,
225   You are but my fellow-mortal!"
      Shawondasee, fat and lazy,—
Had his dwelling far to southward,
In the drowsy, dreamy sunshine,
In the never-ending Summer.
230   He it was who sent the wood-birds,
Sent the Opechee, the robin,
Sent the bluebird, the Owaissa,
Sent the Shawshaw, sent the swallow,
Sent the wild-goose, Wawa, northward,
235   Sent the melons and tobacco,
And the grapes in purple clusters.
      From his pipe the smoke ascending
Filled the sky with haze and vapor,
Filled the air with dreamy softness,
240   Gave a twinkle to the water.
Touched the rugged hills with smoothness,
Brought the tender Indian Summer
To the melancholy North-land,
In the dreary Moon of Snow-shoes.
245   Listless, careless Shawondasee!
In his life he had one shadow,
In his heart one sorrow had he.
Once, as he was gazing northward,

Far away upon a prairie
250 He beheld a maiden standing,
Saw a tall and slender maiden
All alone upon a prairie;
Brightest green were all her garments,
And her hair was like the sunshine.
255   Day by day he gazed upon her,
Day by day he sighed with passion,
Day by day his heart within him
Grew more hot with love and longing
For the maid with yellow tresses.
260 But he was too fat and lazy
To bestir himself and woo her;
Yes, too indolent and easy
To pursue her and persuade her.
So he only gazed upon her,
265 Only sat and sighed with passion
For the maiden of the prairie.
      Till one morning, looking northward,
He beheld her yellow tresses
Changed and covered o'er with whiteness,
270 Covered as with whitest snow-flakes.
"Ah! my brother from the North-land,
From the kingdom of Wabasso,
From the land of the White Rabbit!
You have stolen the maiden from me,
275 You have laid your hand upon her,
You have wooed and won my maiden,
With your stories of the North-land!"
      Thus the wretched Shawondasee
Breathed into the air his sorrow;
280 And the South-Wind o'er the prairie
Wandered warm with sighs of passion,
With the sighs of Shawondasee,
Till the air seemed full of snow-flakes,
Full of thistle-down the prairie,
285 And the maid with hair like sunshine
Vanished from his sight forever;
Never more did Shawondasee
See the maid with yellow tresses!
      Poor, deluded Shawondasee!

290 'T was no woman that you gazed at,
  'T was no maiden that you sighed for,
  'T was the prairie dandelion
  That through all the dreamy Summer
  You had gazed at with such longing,
295 You had sighed for with such passion,
  And had puffed away forever,
  Blown into the air with sighing.
  Ah! deluded Shawondasee!
    Thus the Four Winds were divided;
300 Thus the sons of Mudjekeewis
  Had their stations in the heavens,
  At the corners of the heavens;
  For himself the West-Wind only
  Kept the mighty Mudjekeewis.

III. - HIAWATHA'S CHILDHOOD.

Downward through the evening twilight,
In the days that are forgotten,
In the unremembered ages,
From the full moon fell Nokomis,
5   Fell the beautiful Nokomis,
She a wife but not a mother.
She was sporting with her women,
Swinging in a swing of grape-vines,
When her rival, the rejected,
10   Full of jealousy and hatred,
Cut the leafy swing asunder,
Cut in twain the twisted grape-vines,
And Nokomis fell affrighted
Downward through the evening twilight,
15   On the Muskoday, the meadow,
On the prairie full of blossoms.
"See! a star falls!" said the people;
"From the sky a star is falling!"
    There among the ferns and mosses,
20   There among the prairie lilies,
On the Muskoday, the meadow,

In the moonlight and the starlight,
Fair Nokomis bore a daughter.
And she called her name Wenonah,
25 As the first-born of her daughters.
And the daughter of Nokomis
Grew up like the prairie lilies,
Grew a tall and slender maiden,
With the beauty of the moonlight,
30 With the beauty of the starlight.
    And Nokomis warned her often,
Saying oft, and oft repeating,
"Oh, beware of Mudjekeewis,
Of the West-Wind, Mudjekeewis;
35 Listen not to what he tells you;
Lie not down upon the meadow,
Stoop not down among the lilies,
Lest the West-Wind come and harm you!"
    But she heeded not the warning,
40 Heeded not those words of wisdom.
And the West-Wind came at evening,
Walking lightly o'er the prairie,
Whispering to the leaves and blossoms,
Bending low the flowers and grasses,
45 Found the beautiful Wenonah,
Lying there among the lilies,
Wooed her with his words of sweetness,
Wooed her with his soft caresses,
Till she bore a son in sorrow,
50 Bore a son of love and sorrow,
    Thus was born my Hiawatha,
Thus was born the child of wonder;
But the daughter of Nokomis,
Hiawatha's gentle mother,
55 In her anguish died deserted
By the West-Wind, false and faithless,
By the heartless Mudjekeewis.
    For her daughter, long and loudly
Wailed and wept the sad Nokomis;
60 "Oh that I were dead!" she murmured,
"Oh that I were dead, as thou art!
No more work, and no more weeping,

Wahonowin! Wahonowin!"
      By the shores of Gitche Gumee,
65   By the shining Big-Sea-Water,
Stood the wigwam of Nokomis
Daughter of the Moon, Nokomis.
Dark behind it rose the forest,
Rose the black and gloomy pine-trees,
70   Rose the firs with cones upon them;
Bright before it beat the water,
Beat the clear and sunny water,
Beat the shining Big-Sea-Water.
      There the wrinkled old Nokomis
75   Nursed the little Hiawatha,
Rocked him in his linden cradle,
Bedded soft in moss and rushes,
Safely bound with reindeer sinews;
Stilled his fretful wail by saying,
80   "Hush! the Naked Bear will hear thee!"
Lulled him into slumber, singing,
"Ewa-yea! my little owlet!
Who is this, that lights the wigwam?
With his great eyes lights the wigwam?
85   Ewa-yea! my little owlet!"
      Many things Nokomis taught him
Of the stars that shine in heaven;
Showed him Ishkoodah, the comet,
Ishkoodah, with fiery tresses;
90   Showed the Death-Dance of the spirits,
Warriors with their plumes and war-clubs
Flaring far away to northward
In the frosty nights of Winter;
Showed the broad white road in heaven,
95   Pathway of the ghosts, the shadows,
Running straight across the heavens,
Crowded with the ghosts, the shadows.
      At the door on summer evenings
Sat the little Hiawatha;
100   Heard the whispering of the pine-trees,
Heard the lapping of the waters,
Sounds of music, words of wonder;
"Minne-wawa!" said the pine-trees.

"Mudway-aushka!" said the water.
105   Saw the fire-fly, Wah-wah-taysee,
Flitting through the dusk of evening,
With the twinkle of its candle
Lighting up the brakes and bushes,
And he sang the song of children,
110   Sang the song Nokomis taught him:
"Wah-wah-taysee, little fire-fly,
Little, flitting, white-fire insect,
Little, dancing, white-fire creature,
Light me with your little candle,
115   Ere upon my bed I lay me,
Ere in sleep I close my eyelids!"
       Saw the moon rise from the water
Rippling, rounding from the water,
Saw the flecks and shadows on it,
120   Whispered, "What is that, Nokomis?"
And the good Nokomis answered:
"Once a warrior, very angry,
Seized his grandmother, and threw her
Up into the sky at midnight;
125   Right against the moon he threw her;
'T is her body that you see there."
       Saw the rainbow in the heaven,
In the eastern sky, the rainbow,
Whispered, "What is that, Nokomis?"
130   And the good Nokomis answered:
"'T is the heaven of flowers you see there;
All the wild-flowers of the forest,
All the lilies of the prairie,
When on earth they fade and perish,
135   Blossom in that heaven above us."
       When he heard the owls at midnight,
Hooting, laughing in the forest,
"What is that?" he cried in terror;
"What is that," he said, "Nokomis?"
140   And the good Nokomis answered:
"That is but the owl and owlet,
Talking in their native language,
Talking, scolding at each other."
       Then the little Hiawatha

145   Learned of every bird its language,
Learned their names and all their secrets,
How they built their nests in Summer,
Where they hid themselves in Winter,
Talked with them whene'er he met them,
150   Called them "Hiawatha's Chickens."
        Of all beasts he learned the language,
Learned their names and all their secrets,
How the beavers built their lodges,
Where the squirrels hid their acorns,
155   How the reindeer ran so swiftly,
Why the rabbit was so timid,
Talked with them whene'er he met them,
Called them "Hiawatha's Brothers."
        Then Iagoo, the great boaster,
160   He the marvellous story-teller,
He the traveller and the talker,
He the friend of old Nokomis,
Made a bow for Hiawatha;
From a branch of ash he made it,
165   From an oak-bough made the arrows,
Tipped with flint, and winged with feathers,
And the cord he made of deer-skin.
        Then he said to Hiawatha:
"Go, my son, into the forest,
170   Where the red deer herd together,
Kill for us a famous roebuck,
Kill for us a deer with antlers!"
        Forth into the forest straightway
All alone walked Hiawatha
175   Proudly, with his bow and arrows;
And the birds sang round him, o'er him,
"Do not shoot us, Hiawatha!"
Sang the Opechee, the robin,
Sang the bluebird, the Owaissa,
180   "Do not shoot us, Hiawatha!"
        Up the oak-tree, close beside him,
Sprang the squirrel, Adjidaumo,
In and out among the branches,
Coughed and chattered from the oak-tree,
185   Laughed, and said between his laughing,

"Do not shoot me, Hiawatha!"
And the rabbit from his pathway
Leaped aside, and at a distance
Sat erect upon his haunches,
190   Half in fear and half in frolic,
Saying to the little hunter,
"Do not shoot me, Hiawatha!"
But he heeded not, nor heard them,
For his thoughts were with the red deer;
195   On their tracks his eyes were fastened,
Leading downward to the river,
To the ford across the river,
And as one in slumber walked he.
Hidden in the alder-bushes,
200   There he waited till the deer came,
Till he saw two antlers lifted,
Saw two eyes look from the thicket,
Saw two nostrils point to windward,
And a deer came down the pathway,
205   Flecked with leafy light and shadow.
And his heart within him fluttered,
Trembled like the leaves above him,
Like the birch-leaf palpitated,
As the deer came down the pathway.
210   Then, upon one knee uprising,
Hiawatha aimed an arrow;
Scarce a twig moved with his motion,
Scarce a leaf was stirred or rustled,
But the wary roebuck started,
215   Stamped with all his hoofs together,
Listened with one foot uplifted,
Leaped as if to meet the arrow;
Ah! the singing, fatal arrow;
Like a wasp it buzzed and stung him!
220   Dead he lay there in the forest,
By the ford across the river;
Beat his timid heart no longer,
But the heart of Hiawatha
Throbbed and shouted and exulted,
225   As he bore the red deer homeward,
And Iagoo and Nokomis

Hailed his coming with applauses.
From the red deer's hide Nokomis
Made a cloak for Hiawatha,
230   From the red deer's flesh Nokomis
Made a banquet in his honor.
All the village came and feasted,
All the guests praised Hiawatha,
Called him Strong-Heart, Soan-ge-taha!
Called him Loon-Heart, Mahn-go-taysee!

"I have given you lands to hunt in."

IV. - HIAWATHA AND MUDJEKEEWIS.

Out of childhood into manhood
Now had grown my Hiawatha,
Skilled in all the craft of hunters,
Learned in all the lore of old men,
In all youthful sports and pastimes,
In all manly arts and labors.
Swift of foot was Hiawatha;
He could shoot an arrow from him,
And run forward with such fleetness,
That the arrow fell behind him!
Strong of arm was Hiawatha;
He could shoot ten arrows upward,
Shoot them with such strength and swiftness,
That the tenth had left the bow-string
Ere the first to earth had fallen!
He had mittens, Minjekahwun,
Magic mittens made of deer-skin;
When upon his hands he wore them,
He could smite the rocks asunder,
He could grind them into powder.
He had moccasins enchanted,
Magic moccasins of deer-skin;
When he bound them round his ankles,
When upon his feet he tied them,
At each stride a mile he measured!
Much he questioned old Nokomis
Of his father Mudjekeewis;
Learned from her the fatal secret
Of the beauty of his mother,

30   Of the falsehood of his father;
      And his heart was hot within him,
      Like a living coal his heart was.
              Then he said to old Nokomis,
      "I will go to Mudjekeewis,
35   See how fares it with my father,
      At the doorways of the West-Wind,
      At the portals of the Sunset!"
              From his lodge went Hiawatha,
      Dressed for travel, armed for hunting;
40   Dressed in deer-skin shirt and leggings,
      Richly wrought with quills and wampum
      On his head his eagle-feathers,
      Round his waist his belt of wampum,
      In his hand his bow of ash-wood,
45   Strung with sinews of the reindeer;
      In his quiver oaken arrows,
      Tipped with jasper, winged with feathers;
      With his mittens, Minjekahwun,
      With his moccasins enchanted.
50   Warning said the old Nokomis,
      "Go not forth, O Hiawatha!
      To the kingdom of the West-Wind,
      To the realms of Mudjekeewis,
      Lest he harm you with his magic,
55   Lest he kill you with his cunning!"
              But the fearless Hiawatha
      Heeded not her woman's warning;
      Forth he strode into the forest,
      At each stride a mile he measured;
60   Lurid seemed the sky above him,
      Lurid seemed the earth beneath him,
      Hot and close the air around him,
      Filled with smoke and fiery vapors,
      As of burning woods and prairies.
65   For his heart was hot within him,
      Like a living coal his heart was.
              So he journeyed westward, westward,
      Left the fleetest deer behind him,
      Left the antelope and bison;
70   Crossed the rushing Esconaba,

Crossed the mighty Mississippi,
Passed the Mountains of the Prairie,
Passed the land of Crows and Foxes,
Passed the dwellings of the Blackfeet,
75   Came unto the Rocky Mountains,
To the kingdom of the West-Wind,
Where upon the gusty summits
Sat the ancient Mudjekeewis,
Ruler of the winds of heaven.
80   Filled with awe was Hiawatha
At the aspect of his father.
On the air about him wildly
Tossed and streamed his cloudy tresses,
Gleamed like drifting snow his tresses,
85   Glared like Ishkoodah, the comet,
Like the star with fiery tresses.
           Filled with joy was Mudjekeewis
When he looked on Hiawatha,
Saw his youth rise up before him
90   In the face of Hiawatha,
Saw the beauty of Wenonah
From the grave rise up before him.
           "Welcome!" said he, "Hiawatha,
To the kingdom of the West-Wind!
95   Long have I been waiting for you!
Youth is lovely, age is lonely,
Youth is fiery, age is frosty;
You bring back the days departed,
You bring back my youth of passion,
100   And the beautiful Wenonah!"
           Many days they talked together,
Questioned, listened, waited, answered;
Much the mighty Mudjekeewis
Boasted of his ancient prowess,
105   Of his perilous adventures,
His indomitable courage,
His invulnerable body.
           Patiently sat Hiawatha,
Listening to his father's boasting;
110   With a smile he sat and listened,
Uttered neither threat nor menace,

Neither word nor look betrayed him,
But his heart was hot within him,
Like a living coal his heart was.
115   Then he said, "O Mudjekeewis,
Is there nothing that can harm you?
Nothing that you are afraid of?"
And the mighty Mudjekeewis,
Grand and gracious in his boasting,
120 Answered, saying, "There is nothing,
Nothing but the black rock yonder,
Nothing but the fatal Wawbeek!"
        And he looked at Hiawatha
With a wise look and benignant,
125 With a countenance paternal,
Looked with pride upon the beauty
Of his tall and graceful figure,
Saying, "O my Hiawatha!
Is there anything can harm you?
130 Anything you are afraid of?"
        But the wary Hiawatha
Paused awhile, as if uncertain,
Held his peace, as if resolving,
And then answered, "There is nothing,
135 Nothing but the bulrush yonder,
Nothing but the great Apukwa!"
        And as Mudjekeewis, rising,
Stretched his hand to pluck the bulrush,
Hiawatha cried in terror,
140 Cried in well-dissembled terror,
"Kago! kago! do not touch it!"
"Ah, kaween!" said Mudjekeewis,
"No indeed, I will not touch it!"
        Then they talked of other matters;
145 First of Hiawatha's brothers,
First of Wabun, of the East-Wind,
Of the South-Wind, Shawondasee,
Of the North, Kabibonokka;
Then of Hiawatha's mother,
150 Of the beautiful Wenonah,
Of her birth upon the meadow,
Of her death, as old Nokomis

Had remembered and related.
　　　And he cried, "O Mudjekeewis,
155　It was you who killed Wenonah,
Took her young life and her beauty,
Broke the Lily of the Prairie,
Trampled it beneath your footsteps;
You confess it! you confess it!"
160　And the mighty Mudjekeewis
Tossed his gray hairs to the West-Wind,
Bowed his hoary head in anguish,
With a silent nod assented.

"He was dressed in deer-skin leggings,
Fringed with hedge-hog quills and ermine."
　　　Then up started Hiawatha,
165　And with threatening look and gesture
Laid his hand upon the black rock,
On the fatal Wawbeek laid it,
With his mittens, Minjekahwun,

Rent the jutting crag asunder,
170 Smote and crushed it into fragments,
Hurled them madly at his father,
The remorseful Mudjekeewis,
For his heart was hot within him,
Like a living coal his heart was.
175 But the ruler of the West-Wind
Blew the fragments backward from him,
With the breathing of his nostrils,
With the tempest of his anger,
Blew them back at his assailant;
180 Seized the bulrush, the Apukwa,
Dragged it with its roots and fibres
From the margin of the meadow,
From its ooze, the giant bulrush;
Long and loud laughed Hiawatha!
185 Then began the deadly conflict,
Hand to hand among the mountains;
From his eyry screamed the eagle,
The Keneu, the great war-eagle,
Sat upon the crags around them,
190 Wheeling flapped his wings above them.
Like a tall tree in the tempest
Bent and lashed the giant bulrush;
And in masses huge and heavy
Crashing fell the fatal Wawbeek;
195 Till the earth shook with the tumult
And confusion of the battle,
And the air was full of shoutings,
And the thunder of the mountains,
Starting, answered, "Baim-wawa!"
200 Back retreated Mudjekeewis,
Rushing westward o'er the mountains,
Stumbling westward down the mountains
Three whole days retreated fighting,
Still pursued by Hiawatha
205 To the doorways of the West-Wind,
To the portals of the Sunset,
To the earth's remotest border,
Where into the empty spaces
Sinks the sun, as a flamingo

210 Drops into her nest at nightfall,
In the melancholy marshes.
  "Hold!" at length cried Mudjekeewis,
"Hold, my son, my Hiawatha!
'T is impossible to kill me,
215 For you cannot kill the immortal.
I have put you to this trial,
But to know and prove your courage;
Now receive the prize of valor!
  "Go back to your home and people,
220 Live among them, toil among them,
Cleanse the earth from all that harms it,
Clear the fishing-grounds and rivers,
Slay all monsters and magicians,
All the giants, the Wendigoes,
225 All the serpents, the Kenabeeks,
As I slew the Mishe-Mokwa,
Slew the Great Bear of the mountains.
  "And at last when Death draws near you,
When the awful eyes of Pauguk
230 Glare upon you in the darkness,
I will share my kingdom with you,
Ruler shall you be thenceforward
Of the Northwest-Wind, Keewaydin,
Of the home-wind, the Keewaydin."
235   Thus was fought that famous battle
In the dreadful days of Shah-shah,
In the days long since departed,
In the kingdom of the West-Wind.
Still the hunter sees its traces
240 Scattered far o'er hill and valley;
Sees the giant bulrush growing
By the ponds and water-courses,
Sees the masses of the Wawbeek
Lying still in every valley.
245   Homeward now went Hiawatha;
Pleasant was the landscape round him,
Pleasant was the air above him,
For the bitterness of anger
Had departed wholly from him,
250 From his brain the thought of vengeance,

34

From his heart the burning fever.
      Only once his pace he slackened,
Only once he paused or halted,
Paused to purchase heads of arrows
255   Of the ancient Arrow-maker,
In the land of the Dacotahs,
Where the Falls of Minnehaha
Flash and gleam among the oak-trees,
Laugh and leap into the valley.
260   There the ancient Arrow-maker
Made his arrow-heads of sandstone,
Arrow-heads of chalcedony,
Arrow-heads of flint and jasper,
Smoothed and sharpened at the edges,
265   Hard and polished, keen and costly.
      With him dwelt his dark-eyed daughter,
Wayward as the Minnehaha,
With her moods of shade and sunshine,
Eyes that smiled and frowned alternate,
270   Feet as rapid as the river,
Tresses flowing like the water,
And as musical a laughter;
And he named her from the river,
From the water-fall he named her,
275   Minnehaha, Laughing Water.
      Was it then for heads of arrows,
Arrow-heads of chalcedony,
Arrow-heads of flint and jasper,
That my Hiawatha halted
280   In the land of the Dacotahs?
      Was it not to see the maiden,
See the face of Laughing Water
Peeping from behind the curtain,
Hear the rustling of her garments
285   From behind the waving curtain,
As one sees the Minnehaha
Gleaming, glancing through the branches,
As one hears the Laughing Water
From behind its screen of branches?
290   Who shall say what thoughts and visions
Fill the fiery brains of young men?

Who shall say what dreams of beauty
Filled the heart of Hiawatha?
All he told to old Nokomis,
295   When he reached the lodge at sunset,
Was the meeting with his father,
Was his fight with Mudjekeewis;
Not a word he said of arrows,
Not a word of Laughing Water!

"Blanket Woven by Navajo Woman."

V. - HIAWATHA'S FASTING.

You shall hear how Hiawatha
Prayed and fasted in the forest,
Not for greater skill in hunting,
Not for greater craft in fishing,
5   Not for triumphs in the battle,
And renown among the warriors,
But for profit of the people,
For advantage of the nations.
First he built a lodge for fasting,
10   Built a wigwam in the forest,
By the shining Big-Sea-Water,
In the blithe and pleasant Spring-time,
In the Moon of Leaves he built it,
And, with dreams and visions many,
15   Seven whole days and nights he fasted.
      On the first day of his fasting
Through the leafy woods he wandered;
Saw the deer start from the thicket,
Saw the rabbit in his burrow,
20   Heard the pheasant, Bena, drumming,
Heard the squirrel, Adjidaumo,
Rattling in his hoard of acorns,
Saw the pigeon, the Omeme,
Building nests among the pine-trees,
25   And in flocks the wild goose, Wawa,
Flying to the fen-lands northward,
Whirring, wailing far above him.
"Master of Life!" he cried, desponding,
"Must our lives depend on these things?"

30   On the next day of his fasting
      By the river's brink he wandered,
      Through the Muskoday, the meadow,
      Saw the wild rice, Mahnomonee,
      Saw the blueberry, Meenahga,
35   And the strawberry, Odahmin,
      And the gooseberry, Shahbomin,
      And the grape-vine, the Bemahgut,
      Trailing o'er the alder-branches,
      Filling all the air with fragrance!
40   "Master of Life!" he cried, desponding,
      "Must our lives depend on these things?"
      On the third day of his fasting
      By the lake he sat and pondered,
      By the still, transparent water;
45   Saw the sturgeon, Nahma, leaping,
      Scattering drops like beads of wampum,
      Saw the yellow perch, the Sahwa,
      Like a sunbeam in the water,
      Saw the pike, the Maskenozha,
50   And the herring, Okahahwis,
      And the Shawgashee, the craw-fish!
      "Master of Life!" he cried, desponding,
      "Must our lives depend on these things?"
      On the fourth day of his fasting
55   In his lodge he lay exhausted;
      From his couch of leaves and branches
      Gazing with half-open eyelids,
      Full of shadowy dreams and visions,
      On the dizzy, swimming landscape,
60   On the gleaming of the water,
      On the splendor of the sunset.
      And he saw a youth approaching,
      Dressed in garments green and yellow,
      Coming through the purple twilight,
65   Through the splendor of the sunset;
      Plumes of green bent o'er his forehead,
      And his hair was soft and golden.
      Standing at the open doorway,
      Long he looked at Hiawatha,
70   Looked with pity and compassion

On his wasted form and features,
And, in accents like the sighing
Of the South-Wind in the tree-tops,
Said he, "O my Hiawatha!
75 All your prayers are heard in heaven,
For you pray not like the others;
Not for greater skill in hunting,
Not for greater craft in fishing,
Not for triumph in the battle,
80 Nor renown among the warriors,
But for profit of the people,
For advantage of the nations.
    "From the Master of Life descending,
I, the friend of man, Mondamin,
85 Come to warn you and instruct you,
How by struggle and by labor
You shall gain what you have prayed for.
Rise up from your bed of branches,
Rise, O youth, and wrestle with me!"
90   Faint with famine, Hiawatha
Started from his bed of branches,
From the twilight of his wigwam
Forth into the flush of sunset
Came, and wrestled with Mondamin;
95 At his touch he felt new courage
Throbbing in his brain and bosom,
Felt new life and hope and vigor
Run through every nerve and fibre.
    So they wrestled there together
100 In the glory of the sunset,
And the more they strove and struggled,
Stronger still grew Hiawatha;
Till the darkness fell around them,
And the heron, the Shuh-shuh-gah,
105 From her haunts among the fen-lands,
Gave a cry of lamentation,
Gave a scream of pain and famine.
    "'T is enough!" then said Mondamin,
Smiling upon Hiawatha,
110 "But tomorrow, when the sun sets,
I will come again to try you."

And he vanished, and was seen not;
Whether sinking as the rain sinks,
Whether rising as the mists rise,
115   Hiawatha saw not, knew not,
Only saw that he had vanished,
Leaving him alone and fainting,
With the misty lake below him,
And the reeling stars above him.
120   On the morrow and the next day,
When the sun through heaven descending,
Like a red and burning cinder
From the hearth of the Great Spirit,
Fell into the western waters,
125   Came Mondamin for the trial,
For the strife with Hiawatha;
Came as silent as the dew comes,
From the empty air appearing,
Into empty air returning,
130   Taking shape when earth it touches
But invisible to all men
In its coming and its going.
        Thrice they wrestled there together
In the glory of the sunset,
135   Till the darkness fell around them,
Till the heron, the Shuh-shuh-gah,
From her haunts among the fen-lands,
Uttered her loud cry of famine,
And Mondamin paused to listen.
140   Tall and beautiful he stood there,
In his garments green and yellow;
To and fro his plumes above him
Waved and nodded with his breathing,
And the sweat of the encounter
145   Stood like drops of dew upon him.
        And he cried, "O Hiawatha!
Bravely have you wrestled with me,
Thrice have wrestled stoutly with me,
And the Master of Life, who sees us,
150   He will give to you the triumph!"
        Then he smiled and said: "To-morrow
Is the last day of your conflict,

Is the last day of your fasting.
You will conquer and o'ercome me;
155   Make a bed for me to lie in,
Where the rain may fall upon me,
Where the sun may come and warm me;
Strip these garments, green and yellow,
Strip this nodding plumage from me,
160   Lay me in the earth and make it
Soft and loose and light above me.
         "Let no hand disturb my slumber,
Let no weed nor worm molest me,
Let not Kahgahgee, the raven,
165   Come to haunt me and molest me,
Only come yourself to watch me,
Till I wake, and start, and quicken,
Till I leap into the sunshine."
         And thus saying, he departed;
170   Peacefully slept Hiawatha,
But he heard the Wawonaissa,
Heard the whippoorwill complaining,
Perched upon his lonely wigwam;
Heard the rushing Sebowisha,
175   Heard the rivulet rippling near him,
Talking to the darksome forest;
Heard the sighing of the branches,
As they lifted and subsided
At the passing of the night-wind,
180   Heard them, as one hears in slumber
Far-off murmurs, dreamy whispers:
Peacefully slept Hiawatha.
         On the morrow came Nokomis,
On the seventh day of his fasting,
185   Came with food for Hiawatha,
Came imploring and bewailing,
Lest his hunger should o'ercome him,
Lest his fasting should be fatal.
         But he tasted not, and touched not,
190   Only said to her, "Nokomis,
Wait until the sun is setting,
Till the darkness falls around us,
Till the heron, the Shuh-shuh-gah,

Crying from the desolate marshes,
195 Tells us that the day is ended."
Homeward weeping went Nokomis,
Sorrowing for her Hiawatha,
Fearing lest his strength should fail him,
Lest his fasting should be fatal.
200 He meanwhile sat weary waiting
For the coming of Mondamin,
Till the shadows, pointing eastward,
Lengthened over field and forest,
Till the sun dropped from the heaven,
205 Floating on the waters westward,
As a red leaf in the Autumn
Falls and floats upon the water,
Falls and sinks into its bosom.
And behold! the young Mondamin,
210 With his soft and shining tresses,
With his garments green and yellow,
With his long and glossy plumage,
Stood and beckoned at the doorway.
And as one in slumber walking,
215 Pale and haggard, but undaunted,
From the wigwam Hiawatha
Came and wrestled with Mondamin.
Round about him spun the landscape,
Sky and forest reeled together,
220 And his strong heart leaped within him,
As the sturgeon leaps and struggles
In a net to break its meshes.
Like a ring of fire around him
Blazed and flared the red horizon,
225 And a hundred suns seemed looking
At the combat of the wrestlers.
Suddenly upon the greensward
All alone stood Hiawatha,
Panting with his wild exertion,
230 Palpitating with the struggle;
And before him, breathless, lifeless,
Lay the youth, with hair dishevelled,
Plumage torn, and garments tattered,
Dead he lay there in the sunset.

235   And victorious Hiawatha
Made the grave as he commanded,
Stripped the garments from Mondamin,
Stripped his tattered plumage from him,
Laid him in the earth, and made it
240 Soft and loose and light above him;
And the heron, the Shuh-shuh-gah,
From the melancholy moorlands,
Gave a cry of lamentation,
Gave a cry of pain and anguish!
245   Homeward then went Hiawatha
To the lodge of old Nokomis,
And the seven days of his fasting
Were accomplished and completed.
But the place was not forgotten
250 Where he wrestled with Mondamin;
Nor forgotten nor neglected
Was the grave where lay Mondamin,
Sleeping in the rain and sunshine,
Where his scattered plumes and garments
255 Faded in the rain and sunshine.
           Day by day did Hiawatha
Go to wait and watch beside it;
Kept the dark mould soft above it,
Kept it clean from weeds and insects,
260 Drove away, with scoffs and shoutings,
Kahgahgee, the king of ravens.
           Till at length a small green feather
From the earth shot slowly upward,
Then another and another,
265 And before the Summer ended
Stood the maize in all its beauty,
With its shining robes about it,
And its long, soft, yellow tresses;
And in rapture Hiawatha
270 Cried aloud, "It is Mondamin!
Yes, the friend of man, Mondamin!"
Then he called to old Nokomis
And Iagoo, the great boaster,
Showed them where the maize was growing,
275 Told them of his wondrous vision,

Of his wrestling and his triumph,
Of this new gift to the nations,
Which should be their food forever.
    And still later, when the Autumn
280   Changed the long, green leaves to yellow,
And the soft and juicy kernels
Grew like wampum hard and yellow,
Then the ripened ears he gathered,
Stripped the withered husks from off them,
285   As he once had stripped the wrestler,
Gave the first Feast of Mondamin,
And made known unto the people
This new gift of the Great Spirit.

Comanche Baskets and Pappoose Cradles.

VI. - HIAWATHA'S FRIENDS.

Two good friends had Hiawatha,
Singled out from all the others,
Bound to him in closest union,
And to whom he gave the right hand
5   Of his heart, in joy and sorrow;
Chibiabos, the musician,
And the very strong man, Kwasind.
      Straight between them ran the pathway,
Never grew the grass upon it;
10   Singing birds, that utter falsehoods,
Story-tellers, mischief-makers,
Found no eager ear to listen,
Could not breed ill-will between them,
For they kept each other's counsel,
15   Spake with naked hearts together,
Pondering much and much contriving
How the tribes of men might prosper.
      Most beloved by Hiawatha
Was the gentle Chibiabos,
20   He the best of all musicians,
He the sweetest of all singers.
Beautiful and childlike was he,
Brave as man is, soft as woman,
Pliant as a wand of willow,
25   Stately as a deer with antlers.
      When he sang, the village listened;
All the warriors gathered round him,
All the women came to hear him;
Now he stirred their souls to passion,

30   Now he melted them to pity.
                From the hollow reeds he fashioned
        Flutes so musical and mellow,
        That the brook, the Sebowisha,
        Ceased to murmur in the woodland,
35   That the wood-birds ceased from singing,
        And the squirrel, Adjidaumo,
        Ceased his chatter in the oak-tree,
        And the rabbit, the Wabasso,
        Sat upright to look and listen.
40   Yes, the brook, the Sebowisha,
        Pausing, said, "O Chibiabos,
        Teach my waves to flow in music,
        Softly as your words in singing!"
                Yes, the bluebird, the Owaissa,
45   Envious, said, "O Chibiabos,
        Teach me tones as wild and wayward,
        Teach me songs as full of frenzy!"
                Yes, the Opechee, the robin,
        Joyous, said, "O Chibiabos,
50   Teach me tones as sweet and tender,
        Teach me songs as full of gladness!"
                And the whippoorwill, Wawonaissa,
        Sobbing, said, "O Chibiabos,
        Teach me tones as melancholy,
55   Teach me songs as full of sadness!"
                All the many sounds of nature
        Borrowed sweetness from his singing;
        All the hearts of men were softened
        By the pathos of his music;
60   For he sang of peace and freedom,
        Sang of beauty, love, and longing;
        Sang of death, and life undying
        In the Islands of the Blessed,
        In the kingdom of Ponemah,
65   In the land of the Hereafter.
                Very dear to Hiawatha
        Was the gentle Chibiabos,
        He the best of all musicians,
        He the sweetest of all singers;
70   For his gentleness he loved him,

46

And the magic of his singing.

Dear, too, unto Hiawatha
Was the very strong man, Kwasind,
He the strongest of all mortals,
75   He the mightiest among many;
For his very strength he loved him,
For his strength allied to goodness.
       Idle in his youth was Kwasind,
Very listless, dull, and dreamy,
80   Never played with other children,
Never fished and never hunted,
Not like other children was he;
But they saw that much he fasted,
Much his Manito entreated,
85   Much besought his Guardian Spirit.
       "Lazy Kwasind!" said his mother,
"In my work you never help me!
In the Summer you are roaming
Idly in the fields and forests;
90   In the Winter you are cowering
O'er the firebrands in the wigwam!
In the coldest days of Winter
I must break the ice for fishing;
With my nets you never help me!
95   At the door my nets are hanging,
Dripping, freezing with the water;
Go and wring them, Yenadizze!
Go and dry them in the sunshine!"
       Slowly, from the ashes, Kwasind
100   Rose, but made no angry answer;
From the lodge went forth in silence,
Took the nets, that hung together,
Dripping, freezing at the doorway;
Like a wisp of straw he wrung them,
105   Like a wisp of straw he broke them,
Could not wring them without breaking,
Such the strength was in his fingers.
       "Lazy Kwasind!" said his father,

"In the hunt you never help me;
110   Every bow you touch is broken,
Snapped asunder every arrow;
Yet come with me to the forest,
You shall bring the hunting homeward."
    Down a narrow pass they wandered,
115   Where a brooklet led them onward,
Where the trail of deer and bison
Marked the soft mud on the margin,
Till they found all further passage
Shut against them, barred securely
120   By the trunks of trees uprooted,
Lying lengthwise, lying crosswise,
And forbidding further passage.
    "We must go back," said the old man,
"O'er these logs we cannot clamber;

125   Not a woodchuck could get through them,

Not a squirrel clamber o'er them!"
And straightway his pipe he lighted,
And sat down to smoke and ponder.
But before his pipe was finished,
130   Lo! the path was cleared before him:
All the trunks had Kwasind lifted,
To the right hand, to the left hand,
Shot the pine-trees swift as arrows,
Hurled the cedars light as lances.
135   "Lazy Kwasind!" said the young men,
As they sported in the meadow;
"Why standing idly looking at us,
Leaning on the rock behind you?
Come and wrestle with the others,
140   Let us pitch the quoit together!"
        Lazy Kwasind made no answer,
To their challenge made no answer,
Only rose, and, slowly turning,
Seized the huge rock in his fingers,
145   Tore it from its deep foundation,
Poised it in the air a moment,
Pitched it sheer into the river,
Sheer into the swift Pauwating,
Where it still is seen in Summer.
150   Once as down that foaming river,
Down the rapids of Pauwating,
Kwasind sailed with his companions,
In the stream he saw a beaver,
Saw Ahmeek, the King of Beavers,
155   Struggling with the rushing currents,
Rising, sinking in the water.
        Without speaking, without pausing,
Kwasind leaped into the river,
Plunged beneath the bubbling surface,
160   Through the whirlpools chased the beaver,
Followed him among the islands,
Stayed so long beneath the water,
That his terrified companions
Cried, "Alas! good-by to Kwasind!
165   We shall never more see Kwasind!"
But he reappeared triumphant,

And upon his shining shoulders
Brought the beaver, dead and dripping,
Brought the King of all the Beavers.
170   And these two, as I have told you,
Were the friends of Hiawatha,
Chibiabos, the musician,
And the very strong man, Kwasind.
Long they lived in peace together,
175   Spake with naked hearts together,
Pondering much and much contriving
How the tribes of men might prosper.

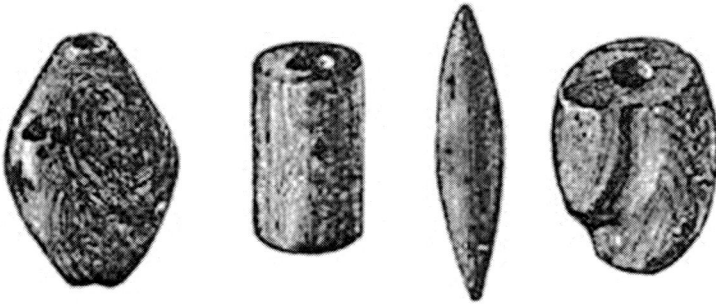

Beads of Wampum, Shells and Turquoise.

VII. - HIAWATHA'S SAILING

Give me of your bark, O Birch-Tree!
Of your yellow bark, O Birch-Tree!
Growing by the rushing river,
Tall and stately in the valley!
5   I a light canoe will build me,
Build a swift Cheemaun for sailing,
That shall float upon the river,
Like a yellow leaf in Autumn,
Like a yellow water-lily!
10   "Lay aside your cloak, O Birch-Tree!
Lay aside your white-skin wrapper,
For the summer-time is coming,
And the sun is warm in heaven,
And you need no white-skin wrapper!"
15   Thus aloud cried Hiawatha
In the solitary forest,
By the rushing Taquamenaw,

When the birds were singing gayly,
In the Moon of Leaves were singing,
20   And the sun, from sleep awaking,
Started up and said, "Behold me!
Gheezis, the great Sun, behold me!"
    And the tree with all its branches
Rustled in the breeze of morning,
25   Saying, with a sigh of patience,
"Take my cloak, O Hiawatha!"
    With his knife the tree he girdled;
Just beneath its lowest branches,
Just above the roots, he cut it,
30   Till the sap came oozing outward;
Down the trunk, from top to bottom,
Sheer he cleft the bark asunder,
With a wooden wedge he raised it,
Stripped it from the trunk unbroken.
35   "Give me of your boughs, O Cedar!
Of your strong and pliant branches,
My canoe to make more steady,
Make more strong and firm beneath me!"
    Through the summit of the Cedar
40   Went a sound, a cry of horror,
Went a murmur of resistance;
But it whispered, bending downward,
"Take my boughs, O Hiawatha!"
    Down he hewed the boughs of cedar,
45   Shaped them straightway to a framework,
Like two bows he formed and shaped them,
Like two bended bows together.
    "Give me of your roots, O Tamarack!
Of your fibrous roots, O Larch-Tree!
50   My canoe to bind together,
So to bind the ends together
That the water may not enter,
That the river may not wet me!"
    And the Larch, with all its fibres,
55   Shivered in the air of morning,
Touched his forehead with its tassels,
Said, with one long sigh of sorrow,
"Take them all, O Hiawatha!"

From the earth he tore the fibres,
60 Tore the tough roots of the Larch-Tree,
Closely sewed the bark together,
Bound it closely to the framework.
          "Give me of your balm, O Fir-Tree!
Of your balsam and your resin,
65 So to close the seams together
That the water may not enter,
That the river may not wet me!"
          And the Fir-Tree, tall and sombre,
Sobbed through all its robes of darkness,
70 Rattled like a shore with pebbles,
Answered wailing, answered weeping,
"Take my balm, O Hiawatha!"
          And he took the tears of balsam,
Took the resin of the Fir-Tree,
75 Smeared therewith each seam and fissure,
Made each crevice safe from water.
          "Give me of your quills, O Hedgehog!
All your quills, O Kagh, the Hedgehog!
I will make a necklace of them,
80 Make a girdle for my beauty,
And two stars to deck her bosom!"
          From a hollow tree the Hedgehog
With his sleepy eyes looked at him,
Shot his shining quills, like arrows,
85 Saying, with a drowsy murmur,
Through the tangle of his whiskers,
"Take my quills, O Hiawatha!"
          From the ground the quills he gathered,
All the little shining arrows,
90 Stained them red and blue and yellow,
With the juice of roots and berries;
Into his canoe he wrought them,
Round its waist a shining girdle,
Round its bows a gleaming necklace,
95 On its breast two stars resplendent.

Thus the Birch Canoe was builded
In the valley, by the river,
In the bosom of the forest;
And the forest's life was in it,
100   All its mystery and its magic,
All the lightness of the birch-tree,
All the toughness of the cedar,
All the larch's supple sinews;
And it floated on the river,
105   Like a yellow leaf in Autumn,
Like a yellow water-lily.
       Paddles none had Hiawatha,
Paddles none he had or needed,
For his thoughts as paddles served him,
110   And his wishes served to guide him;
Swift or slow at will he glided,
Veered to right or left at pleasure.
       Then he called aloud to Kwasind,
To his friend, the strong man, Kwasind,
115   Saying, "Help me clear this river
Of its sunken logs and sand-bars,"
       Straight into the river Kwasind
Plunged as if he were an otter,
Dived as if he were a beaver,
120   Stood up to his waist in water,

To his arm-pits in the river,
Swam and shouted in the river,
Tugged at sunken logs and branches,
With his hands he scooped the sand-bars,
125   With his feet the ooze and tangle.

And thus sailed my Hiawatha
Down the rushing Taquamenaw,
Sailed through all its bends and windings,
Sailed through all its deeps and shallows,
130   While his friend, the strong man, Kwasind,
Swam the deeps, the shallows waded.
Up and down the river went they,
In and out among its islands,
Cleared its bed of root and sand-bar,
135   Dragged the dead trees from its channel,

Made its passage safe and certain,
Made a pathway for the people,
From its springs among the mountains,
To the waters of Pauwating,
140   To the bay of Taquamenaw.

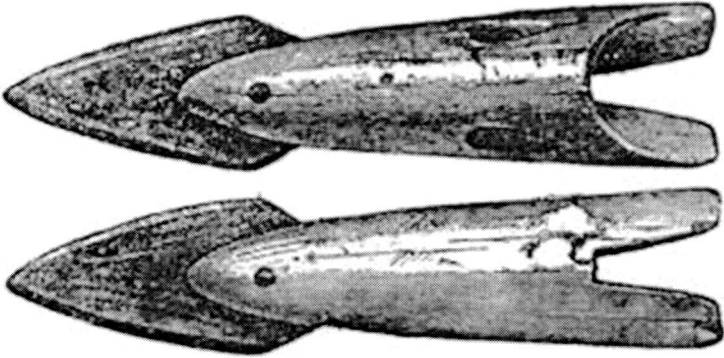

Flint Heads of Ojibway Fish-Spears.

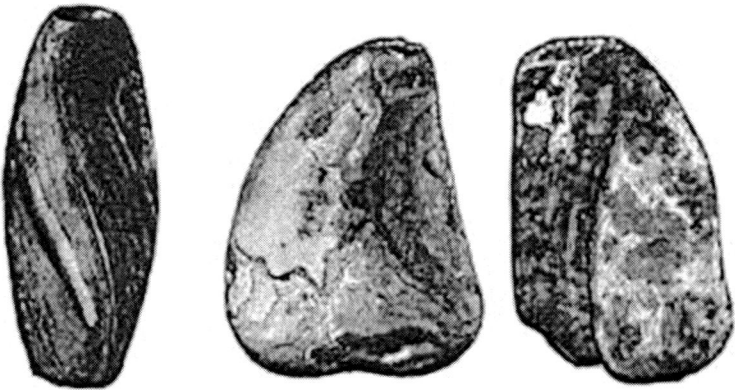

Shell and Pearl Beads of the Iroquois.

VIII. - HIAWATHA'S FISHING.

Forth upon the Gitche Gumee,
On the shining Big-Sea-Water,
With his fishing-line of cedar,
Of the twisted bark of cedar,
5 Forth to catch the sturgeon Nahma,
Mishe-Nahma, King of Fishes,
In his birch canoe exulting
All alone went Hiawatha.
Through the clear, transparent water
10 He could see the fishes swimming
Far down in the depths below him;
See the yellow perch, the Sahwa,
Like a sunbeam in the water,
See the Shawgashee, the craw-fish,
15 Like a spider on the bottom,
On the white and sandy bottom.
At the stern sat Hiawatha,
With his fishing-line of cedar;
In his plumes the breeze of morning
20 Played as in the hemlock branches;
On the bows, with tail erected,
Sat the squirrel, Adjidaumo;
In his fur the breeze of morning
Played as in the prairie grasses.
25 On the white sand of the bottom
Lay the monster Mishe-Nahma,
Lay the sturgeon, King of Fishes;
Through his gills he breathed the water,
With his fins he fanned and winnowed,

30 With his tail he swept the sand-floor.
    There he lay in all his armor;
 On each side a shield to guard him,
 Plates of bone upon his forehead,
 Down his sides and back and shoulders
35 Plates of bone with spines projecting,
 Painted was he with his war-paints,
 Stripes of yellow, red, and azure,
 Spots of brown and spots of sable;
 And he lay there on the bottom,
40 Fanning with his fins of purple,
 As above him Hiawatha
 In his birch canoe came sailing,
 With his fishing-line of cedar.
    "Take my bait!" cried Hiawatha,
45 Down into the depths beneath him,
 "Take my bait, O Sturgeon, Nahma!
 Come up from below the water,
 Let us see which is the stronger!"
 And he dropped his line of cedar
50 Through the clear, transparent water,
 Waited vainly for an answer,
 Long sat waiting for an answer,
 And repeating loud and louder,
 "Take my bait, O King of Fishes!"
55   Quiet lay the sturgeon, Nahma,
 Fanning slowly in the water,
 Looking up at Hiawatha,
 Listening to his call and clamor,
 His unnecessary tumult,
60 Till he wearied of the shouting;
 And he said to the Kenozha,
 To the pike, the Maskenozha,
 "Take the bait of this rude fellow,
 Break the line of Hiawatha!"
65   In his fingers Hiawatha
 Felt the loose line jerk and tighten;
 As he drew it in, it tugged so,
 That the birch canoe stood endwise,
 Like a birch log in the water,
70 With the squirrel, Adjidaumo,

Perched and frisking on the summit.

          Full of scorn was Hiawatha
When he saw the fish rise upward,
Saw the pike, the Maskenozha,
75   Coming nearer, nearer to him,
And he shouted through the water,
"Esa! esa! shame upon you!
You are but the pike, Kenozha,
You are not the fish I wanted,
80   You are not the King of Fishes!"
          Reeling downward to the bottom
Sank the pike in great confusion,
And the mighty sturgeon, Nahma,
Said to Ugudwash, the sun-fish,
85   "Take the bait of this great boaster,
Break the line of Hiawatha!"
          Slowly upward, wavering, gleaming,

Like a white moon in the water;
Rose the Ugudwash, the sun-fish,
90   Seized the line of Hiawatha,
Swung with all his weight upon it,
Made a whirlpool in the water,
Whirled the birch canoe in circles,
Round and round in gurgling eddies,
95   Till the circles in the water
Reached the far-off sandy beaches,
Till the water-flags and rushes
Nodded on the distant margins.
      But when Hiawatha saw him
100   Slowly rising through the water,
Lifting his great disc of whiteness,
Loud he shouted in derision,
"Esa! esa! shame upon you!
You are Ugudwash, the sun-fish,
105   You are not the fish I wanted,
You are not the King of Fishes!"
      Wavering downward, white and ghastly,
Sank the Ugudwash, the sun-fish,
And again the sturgeon, Nahma,
110   Heard the shout of Hiawatha,
Heard his challenge of defiance,
The unnecessary tumult,
Ringing far across the water.
      From the white sand of the bottom
115   Up he rose with angry gesture,
Quivering in each nerve and fibre,
Clashing all his plates of armor,
Gleaming bright with all his war-paint;
In his wrath he darted upward,
120   Flashing leaped into the sunshine,
Opened his great jaws, and swallowed
Both canoe and Hiawatha.
      Down into that darksome cavern
Plunged the headlong Hiawatha,
125   As a log on some black river
Shoots and plunges down the rapids,
Found himself in utter darkness,
Groped around in helpless wonder,

Till he felt a great heart beating,
130   Throbbing in that utter darkness.
          And he smote it in his anger,
With his fist, the heart of Nahma,
Felt the mighty King of Fishes
Shudder through each nerve and fibre,
135   Heard the water gurgle round him
As he leaped and staggered through it,
Sick at heart, and faint and weary.
          Crosswise then did Hiawatha
Drag his birch-canoe for safety,
140   Lest from out the jaws of Nahma,
In the turmoil and confusion,
Forth he might be hurled and perish.
And the squirrel, Adjidaumo,
Frisked and chattered very gayly,
145   Toiled and tugged with Hiawatha
Till the labor was completed.
          Then said Hiawatha to him,
"O my little friend, the squirrel,
Bravely have you toiled to help me;
150   Take the thanks of Hiawatha,
And the name which now he gives you;
For hereafter and forever
Boys shall call you Adjidaumo,
Tail-in-air the boys shall call you!"
155   And again the sturgeon, Nahma,
Gasped and quivered in the water,
Then was still, and drifted landward
Till he grated on the pebbles,
Till the listening Hiawatha
160   Heard him grate upon the margin,
Felt him strand upon the pebbles,
Knew that Nahma, King of Fishes,
Lay there dead upon the margin.
          Then he heard a clang and flapping,
165   As of many wings assembling,
Heard a screaming and confusion,
As of birds of prey contending,
Saw a gleam of light above him,
Shining through the ribs of Nahma,

170   Saw the glittering eyes of sea-gulls,
Of Kayoshk, the sea-gulls, peering,
Gazing at him through the opening,
Heard them saying to each other,
"'T is our brother, Hiawatha!"

175   And he shouted from below them,
Cried exulting from the caverns:
"O ye sea-gulls! O my brothers!
I have slain the sturgeon, Nahma;
Make the rifts a little larger,

180   With your claws the openings widen,
Set me free from this dark prison,
And henceforward and forever
Men shall speak of your achievements,
Calling you Kayoshk, the sea-gulls,

185   Yes, Kayoshk, the Noble Scratchers!"
            And the wild and clamorous sea-gulls
Toiled with beak and claws together,
Made the rifts and openings wider
In the mighty ribs of Nahma,

190   And from peril and from prison,
From the body of the sturgeon,
From the peril of the water,
They released my Hiawatha.
            He was standing near his wigwam,

195   On the margin of the water,
And he called to old Nokomis,
Called and beckoned to Nokomis,
Pointed to the sturgeon, Nahma,
Lying lifeless on the pebbles,

200   With the sea-gulls feeding on him.
            "I have slain the Mishe-Nahma,
Slain the King of Fishes!" said he;
"Look! the sea-gulls feed upon him,
Yes, my friends Kayoshk, the sea-gulls;

205   Drive them not away, Nokomis,
They have saved me from great peril
In the body of the sturgeon,
Wait until their meal is ended,
Till their craws are full with feasting,

210   Till they homeward fly, at sunset,

To their nests among the marshes;
Then bring all your pots and kettles,
And make oil for us in Winter."
                And she waited till the sun set,
215   Till the pallid moon, the Night-sun,
Rose above the tranquil water,
Till Kayoshk, the sated sea-gulls,
From their banquet rose with clamor,
And across the fiery sunset
220   Winged their way to far-off islands,
To their nests among the rushes.
                To his sleep went Hiawatha,
And Nokomis to her labor,
Toiling patient in the moonlight,
225   Till the sun and moon changed places,
Till the sky was red with sunrise,
And Kayoshk, the hungry sea-gulls,
Came back from the reedy islands,
Clamorous for their morning banquet.
230   Three whole days and nights alternate
Old Nokomis and the sea-gulls
Stripped the oily flesh of Nahma,
Till the waves washed through the rib-bones,
Till the sea-gulls came no longer,
235   And upon the sands lay nothing
But the skeleton of Nahma.

Stone Axes of the Blackfeet Indians.

Sioux Indians, in Wolf-Skins, Hunting Buffalo.

IX. - HIAWATHA AND THE PEARL-FEATHER.

On the shores of Gitche Gumee,
Of the shining Big-Sea-Water,
Stood Nokomis, the old woman,
Pointing with her finger westward,
O'er the water pointing westward,
To the purple clouds of sunset.
Fiercely the red sun descending
Burned his way along the heavens,
Set the sky on fire behind him,
As war-parties, when retreating,
Burn the prairies on their war-trail;
And the moon, the Night-sun, eastward,
Suddenly starting from his ambush,
Followed fast those bloody footprints,
Followed in that fiery war-trail,
With its glare upon his features.
      And Nokomis, the old woman,
Pointing with her finger westward,
Spake these words to Hiawatha:
"Yonder dwells the great Pearl-Feather,
Megissogwon, the Magician,
Manito of Wealth and Wampum,
Guarded by his fiery serpents,
Guarded by the black pitch-water.
You can see his fiery serpents,
The Kenabeek, the great serpents,
Coiling, playing in the water;
You can see the black pitch-water

Stretching far away beyond them,
30   To the purple clouds of sunset!
        "He it was who slew my father,
By his wicked wiles and cunning,
When he from the moon descended,
When he came on earth to seek me.
35   He, the mightiest of Magicians,
Sends the fever from the marshes,
Sends the pestilential vapors,
Sends the poisonous exhalations,
Sends the white fog from the fen-lands,
40   Sends disease and death among us!
        "Take your bow, O Hiawatha,
Take your arrows, jasper-headed,
Take your war-club, Puggawaugun,
And your mittens, Minjekahwun,
45   And your birch canoe for sailing,
And the oil of Mishe-Nahma,
So to smear its sides, that swiftly
You may pass the black pitch-water;
Slay this merciless magician,
50   Save the people from the fever
That he breathes across the fen-lands,
And avenge my father's murder!"
        Straightway then my Hiawatha
Armed himself with all his war-gear,
55   Launched his birch canoe for sailing;
With his palm its sides he patted,
Said with glee, "Cheemaun, my darling,
O my Birch-canoe! leap forward,
Where you see the fiery serpents,
60   Where you see the black pitch-water!"
        Forward leaped Cheemaun exulting,
And the Noble Hiawatha
Sang his war-song wild and woful,
And above him the war-eagle,
65   The Keneu, the great war-eagle,
Master of all fowls with feathers,
Screamed and hurtled through the heavens.
        Soon he reached the fiery serpents,
The Kenabeek, the great serpents,

70   Lying huge upon the water,
           Sparkling, rippling in the water,
           Lying coiled across the passage,
           With their blazing crests uplifted,
           Breathing fiery fogs and vapors,
75   So that none could pass beyond them.
               But the fearless Hiawatha
           Cried aloud, and spake in this wise:
           "Let me pass my way, Kenabeek,
           Let me go upon my journey!"
80   And they answered, hissing fiercely,
           With their fiery breath made answer:
           "Back, go back! O Shaugodaya!
           Back to old Nokomis, Faint-heart!"
               Then the angry Hiawatha
85   Raised his mighty bow of ash-tree,

           Seized his arrows, jasper-headed,
           Shot them fast among the serpents;
           Every twanging of the bow-string

Was a war-cry and a death-cry,
90   Every whizzing of an arrow
Was a death-song of Kenabeek.
     Weltering in the bloody water,
Dead lay all the fiery serpents,
And among them Hiawatha
95   Harmless sailed, and cried exulting:
"Onward, O Cheemaun, my darling!
Onward to the black pitch-water!"
     Then he took the oil of Nahma,
And the bows and sides anointed,
100   Smeared them well with oil, that swiftly
He might pass the black pitch-water.
     All night long he sailed upon it,
Sailed upon that sluggish water,
Covered with its mould of ages,
105   Black with rotting water-rushes,
Rank with flags and leaves of lilies,
Stagnant, lifeless, dreary, dismal,
Lighted by the shimmering moonlight,
And by will-o'-the-wisps illumined,
110   Fires by ghosts of dead men kindled,
In their weary night-encampments.
     All the air was white with moonlight,
All the water black with shadow,
And around him the Suggema,
115   The mosquito, sang his war-song,
And the fire-flies, Wah-wah-taysee,
Waved their torches to mislead him;
And the bull-frog, the Dahinda,
Thrust his head into the moonlight,
120   Fixed his yellow eyes upon him,
Sobbed and sank beneath the surface;
And anon a thousand whistles,
Answered over all the fen-lands,
And the heron, the Shuh-shuh-gah,
125   Far off on the reedy margin,
Heralded the hero's coming.
     Westward thus fared Hiawatha,
Toward the realm of Megissogwon,
Toward the land of the Pearl-Feather,

130 Till the level moon stared at him,
In his face stared pale and haggard,
Till the sun was hot behind him,
Till it burned upon his shoulders,
And before him on the upland
135 He could see the Shining Wigwam
Of the Manito of Wampum,
Of the mightiest of Magicians.
    Then once more Cheemaun he patted,
To his birch-canoe said, "Onward!"
140 And it stirred in all its fibres,
And with one great bound of triumph
Leaped across the water-lilies,
Leaped through tangled flags and rushes,
And upon the beach beyond them
145 Dry-shod landed Hiawatha.
    Straight he took his bow of ash-tree,
One end on the sand he rested,
With his knee he pressed the middle,
Stretched the faithful bow-string tighter,
150 Took an arrow, jasper-headed,
Shot it at the Shining Wigwam,
Sent it singing as a herald,
As a bearer of his message,
Of his challenge loud and lofty:
155 "Come forth from your lodge, Pearl-Feather!
Hiawatha waits your coming!"
    Straightway from the Shining Wigwam
Came the mighty Megissogwon,
Tall of stature, broad of shoulder,
160 Dark and terrible in aspect,
Clad from head to foot in wampum,
Armed with all his warlike weapons,
Painted like the sky of morning,
Streaked with crimson, blue and yellow,
165 Crested with great eagle-feathers,
Streaming upward, streaming outward.
    "Well I know you, Hiawatha!"
Cried he in a voice of thunder,
In a tone of loud derision.
170 "Hasten back, O Shaugodaya!

Hasten back among the women,
Back to old Nokomis, Faint-heart!
I will slay you as you stand there,
As of old I slew her father!"
175   But my Hiawatha answered,
Nothing daunted, fearing nothing:
"Big words do not smite like war-clubs,
Boastful breath is not a bow-string,
Taunts are not as sharp as arrows,
180 Deeds are better things than words are,
Actions mightier than boastings!"
   Then began the greatest battle
That the sun had ever looked on,
That the war-birds ever witnessed.
185 All a Summer's day it lasted,
From the sunrise to the sunset;
For the shafts of Hiawatha
Harmless hit the shirt of wampum,
Harmless fell the blows he dealt it
190 With his mittens, Minjekahwun,
Harmless fell the heavy war-club;
It could dash the rocks asunder,
But it could not break the meshes
Of that magic shirt of wampum.
195   Till at sunset Hiawatha,
Leaning on his bow of ash-tree,
Wounded, weary, and desponding,
With his mighty war-club broken,
With his mittens torn and tattered,
200 And three useless arrows only,
Paused to rest beneath a pine-tree,
From whose branches trailed the mosses,
And whose trunk was coated over
With the Dead-man's Moccasin-leather,
205 With the fungus white and yellow.
   Suddenly from the boughs above him
Sang the Mama, the woodpecker:
"Aim your arrows, Hiawatha,
At the head of Megissogwon,
210 Strike the tuft of hair upon it,
At their roots the long black tresses;

There alone can he be wounded!"
     Winged with feathers, tipped with jasper,
Swift flew Hiawatha's arrow,
215   Just as Megissogwon, stooping,
Raised a heavy stone to throw it.
Full upon the crown it struck him,
At the roots of his long tresses,
And he reeled and staggered forward,

220   Plunging like a wounded bison,
Yes, like Pezhekee, the bison,
When the snow is on the prairie.
     Swifter flew the second arrow,
In the pathway of the other,
225   Piercing deeper than the other,
Wounding sorer than the other;
And the knees of Megissogwon
Shook like windy reeds beneath him,
Bent and trembled like the rushes.
230   But the third and latest arrow
Swiftest flew, and wounded sorest,
And the mighty Megissogwon
Saw the fiery eyes of Pauguk,
Saw the eyes of Death glare at him,
235   Heard his voice call in the darkness;
At the feet of Hiawatha
Lifeless lay the great Pearl-Feather,
Lay the mightiest of Magicians.
     Then the grateful Hiawatha

240   Called the Mama, the woodpecker,
    From his perch among the branches
    Of the melancholy pine-tree,
    And, in honor of his service,
    Stained with blood the tuft of feathers
245   On the little head of Mama;
    Even to this day he wears it,
    Wears the tuft of crimson feathers
    As a symbol of his service.
        Then he stripped the shirt of wampum
250   From the back of Megissogwon,
    As a trophy of the battle,
    As a signal of his conquest.
    On the shore he left the body,
    Half on land and half in water,
255   In the sand his feet were buried,
    And his face was in the water.
    And above him, wheeled and clamored
    The Keneu, the great war-eagle,
    Sailing round in narrower circles,
260   Hovering nearer, nearer, nearer.
        From the wigwam Hiawatha
    Bore the wealth of Megissogwon,
    All his wealth of skins and wampum,
    Furs of bison and of beaver,
265   Furs of sable and of ermine,
    Wampum belts and strings and pouches,
    Quivers wrought with beads of wampum,
    Filled with arrows, silver-headed.
        Homeward then he sailed exulting,
270   Homeward through the black pitch-water,
    Homeward through the weltering serpents,
    With the trophies of the battle,
    With a shout and song of triumph.
        On the shore stood old Nokomis,
275   On the shore stood Chibiabos,
    And the very strong man, Kwasind,
    Waiting for the hero's coming,
    Listening to his song of triumph.
    And the people of the village
280   Welcomed him with songs and dances,

Made a joyous feast, and shouted:
"Honor be to Hiawatha!
He has slain the great Pearl-Feather,
Slain the mightiest of Magicians,
285   Him who sent the fiery fever,
Sent the white fog from the fen-lands,
Sent disease and death among us!"
    Ever dear to Hiawatha
Was the memory of Mama!
290   And in token of his friendship,
As a mark of his remembrance,
He adorned and decked his pipe-stem
With the crimson tuft of feathers,
With the blood-red crest of Mama.
295   But the wealth of Megissogwon,
All the trophies of the battle,
He divided with his people,
Shared it equally among them.

Apache Indians Lassoing Wild Horses.

X. - HIAWATHA'S WOOING.

"As unto the bow the cord is,
So unto the man is woman,
Though she bends him, she obeys him,
Though she draws him, yet she follows,
5 Useless each without the other!"
Thus the youthful Hiawatha
Said within himself and pondered,
Much perplexed by various feelings,
Listless, longing, hoping, fearing,
10 Dreaming still of Minnehaha,
Of the lovely Laughing Water,
In the land of the Dacotahs.
  "Wed a maiden of your people,"
Warning said the old Nokomis;
15 "Go not eastward, go not westward,
For a stranger, whom we know not!
Like a fire upon the hearth-stone
Is a neighbor's homely daughter,
Like the starlight or the moonlight
20 Is the handsomest of strangers!"
  Thus dissuading spake Nokomis,
And my Hiawatha answered
Only this: "Dear old Nokomis,
Very pleasant is the firelight,
25 But I like the starlight better,
Better do I like the moonlight!"
  Gravely then said old Nokomis:
"Bring not here an idle maiden,
Bring not here a useless woman,

30 Hands unskilful, feet unwilling;
   Bring a wife with nimble fingers,
   Heart and hand that move together,
   Feet that run on willing errands!"
     Smiling answered Hiawatha:
35 "In the land of the Dacotahs
   Lives the Arrow-maker's daughter,
   Minnehaha, Laughing Water,
   Handsomest of all the women.
   I will bring her to your wigwam,
40 She shall run upon your errands,
   Be your starlight, moonlight, firelight,
   Be the sunlight of my people!"
     Still dissuading said Nokomis:
   "Bring not to my lodge a stranger
45 From the land of the Dacotahs!
   Very fierce are the Dacotahs,
   Often is there war between us,
   There are feuds yet unforgotten,
   Wounds that ache and still may open!"
50   Laughing answered Hiawatha:
   "For that reason, if no other,
   Would I wed the fair Dacotah,
   That our tribes might be united,
   That old feuds might be forgotten,
55 And old wounds be healed forever!"

     Thus departed Hiawatha
   To the land of the Dacotahs,
   To the land of handsome women;
   Striding over moor and meadow,
60 Through interminable forests,
   Through uninterrupted silence.
     With his moccasins of magic,
   At each stride a mile he measured;
   Yet the way seemed long before him,
65 And his heart outrun his footsteps;
   And he journeyed without resting,
   Till he heard the cataract's thunder,

Heard the Falls of Minnehaha
Calling to him through the silence.
70 "Pleasant is the sound!" he murmured,
"Pleasant is the voice that calls me!"
      On the outskirts of the forest,
'Twixt the shadow and the sunshine,
Herds of fallow deer were feeding,
75 But they saw not Hiawatha;
To his bow he whispered, "Fail not!"
To his arrow whispered, "Swerve not!"
Sent it singing on its errand,
To the red heart of the roebuck;
80 Threw the deer across his shoulder,
And sped forward without pausing.
      At the doorway of his wigwam
Sat the ancient Arrow-maker,
In the land of the Dacotahs,
85 Making arrow-heads of jasper,
Arrow-heads of chalcedony.
At his side in all her beauty,
Sat the lovely Minnehaha,
Sat his daughter, Laughing Water,
90 Plaiting mats of flags and rushes;
Of the past the old man's thoughts were,
And the maiden's of the future.
      He was thinking, as he sat there,
Of the days when with such arrows
95 He had struck the deer and bison,
On the Muskoday, the meadow;
Shot the wild goose, flying southward,
On the wing, the clamorous Wawa;
Thinking of the great war-parties,
100 How they came to buy his arrows,
Could not fight without his arrows.
Ah, no more such noble warriors
Could be found on earth as they were!
Now the men were all like women,
105 Only used their tongues for weapons!
      She was thinking of a hunter,
From another tribe and country,
Young and tall and very handsome,

Who one morning, in the Spring-time,
110   Came to buy her father's arrows,
Sat and rested in the wigwam,
Lingered long about the doorway,
Looking back as he departed.
She had heard her father praise him,
115   Praise his courage and his wisdom;
Would he come again for arrows
To the Falls of Minnehaha?
On the mat her hands lay idle,
And her eyes were very dreamy.
120   Through their thoughts they heard a footstep,
Heard a rustling in the branches,
And with glowing cheek and forehead,
With the deer upon his shoulders,
Suddenly from out the woodlands

125 Hiawatha stood before them.
   Straight the ancient Arrow-maker
Looked up gravely from his labor,
Laid aside the unfinished arrow,
Bade him enter at the doorway,
130 Saying, as he rose to meet him,
"Hiawatha, you are welcome!"
   At the feet of Laughing Water
Hiawatha laid his burden,
Threw the red deer from his shoulders;
135 And the maiden looked up at him,
Looked up from her mat of rushes,
Said with gentle look and accent,
"You are welcome, Hiawatha!"
   Very spacious was the wigwam,
140 Made of deer-skin dressed and whitened,
With the Gods of the Dacotahs
Drawn and painted on its curtains,
And so tall the doorway, hardly
Hiawatha stooped to enter,
145 Hardly touched his eagle-feathers
As he entered at the doorway.
   Then uprose the Laughing Water,
From the ground fair Minnehaha,
Laid aside her mat unfinished,
150 Brought forth food and set before them,
Water brought them from the brooklet,
Gave them food in earthen vessels,
Gave them drink in bowls of bass-wood,
Listened while the guest was speaking,
155 Listened while her father answered,
But not once her lips she opened,
Not a single word she uttered.
   Yes, as in a dream she listened
To the words of Hiawatha,
160 As he talked of old Nokomis,
Who had nursed him in his childhood,
As he told of his companions,
Chibiabos, the musician,
And the very strong man, Kwasind,
165 And of happiness and plenty

In the land of the Ojibways,
In the pleasant land and peaceful.
    "After many years of warfare,
Many years of strife and bloodshed,
170   There is peace between the Ojibways
And the tribe of the Dacotahs."
Thus continued Hiawatha,
And then added, speaking slowly,
"That this peace may last forever,
175   And our hands be clasped more closely,
And our hearts be more united,
Give me as my wife this maiden,
Minnehaha, Laughing Water,
Loveliest of Dacotah women!"
180   And the ancient Arrow-maker
Paused a moment ere he answered,
Smoked a little while in silence,
Looked at Hiawatha proudly,
Fondly looked at Laughing Water,
185   And made answer very gravely:
"Yes, if Minnehaha wishes;
Let your heart speak, Minnehaha!"
        And the lovely Laughing Water
Seemed more lovely, as she stood there,
190   Neither willing nor reluctant,
As she went to Hiawatha,
Softly took the seat beside him,
While she said, and blushed to say it,
"I will follow you, my husband!"
195   This was Hiawatha's wooing!
Thus it was he won the daughter
Of the ancient Arrow-maker,
In the land of the Dacotahs!
        From the wigwam he departed,
200   Leading with him Laughing Water;
Hand in hand they went together,
Through the woodland and the meadow,
Left the old man standing lonely
At the doorway of his wigwam,
205   Heard the Falls of Minnehaha
Calling to them from the distance,

Crying to them from afar off,
"Fare thee well, O Minnehaha!"
    And the ancient Arrow-maker
210   Turned again unto his labor,
Sat down by his sunny doorway,
Murmuring to himself, and saying:
"Thus it is our daughters leave us,
Those we love, and those who love us!
215   Just when they have learned to help us,
When we are old and lean upon them,
Comes a youth with flaunting feathers,
With his flute of reeds, a stranger
Wanders piping through the village,
220   Beckons to the fairest maiden,
And she follows where he leads her,
Leaving all things for the stranger!"

    Pleasant was the journey homeward,
Through interminable forests,
225   Over meadow, over mountain,
Over river, hill, and hollow.
Short it seemed to Hiawatha,
Though they journeyed very slowly,
Though his pace he checked and slackened
230   To the steps of Laughing Water.
Who stands on that cliff, like a figure of stone,
        Unmoving and tall in the light of the sky,
        Where the spray of the cataract sparkles on high
All lonely and sternly, save Mogg Megone?
        Over wide and rushing rivers
In his arms he bore the maiden;
Light he thought her as a feather,
As the plume upon his head-gear;
235   Cleared the tangled pathway for her,
Bent aside the swaying branches,
Made at night a lodge of branches,
And a bed with boughs of hemlock,
And a fire before the doorway
240   With the dry cones of the pine-tree.

All the travelling winds went with them,
O'er the meadow, through the forest;
All the stars of night looked at them,
Watched with sleepless eyes their slumber;
245   From his ambush in the oak-tree
Peeped the squirrel, Adjidaumo,
Watched with eager eyes the lovers;
And the rabbit, the Wabasso,
Scampered from the path before them,

250   Peering, peeping from his burrow,
Sat erect upon his haunches,
Watched with curious eyes the lovers.
        Pleasant was the journey homeward!
All the birds sang loud and sweetly
255   Songs of happiness and heart's-ease;
Sang the bluebird, the Owaissa,
"Happy are you, Hiawatha,
Having such a wife to love you!"

Sang the Opechee, the robin,
260   "Happy are you, Laughing Water,
Having such a noble husband!"
    From the sky the sun benignant
Looked upon them through the branches,
Saying to them, "O my children,
265   Love is sunshine, hate is shadow,
Life is checkered shade and sunshine,
Rule by love, O Hiawatha!"
    From the sky the moon looked at them,
Filled the lodge with mystic splendors,
270   Whispered to them, "O my children,
Day is restless, night is quiet,
Man imperious, woman feeble;
Half is mine, although I follow;
Rule by patience, Laughing Water!"
275   Thus it was they journeyed homeward;
Thus it was that Hiawatha
To the lodge of old Nokomis
Brought the moonlight, starlight, firelight,
Brought the sunshine of his people,
280   Minnehaha, Laughing Water,
Handsomest of all the women
In the land of the Dacotahs,
In the land of handsome women.

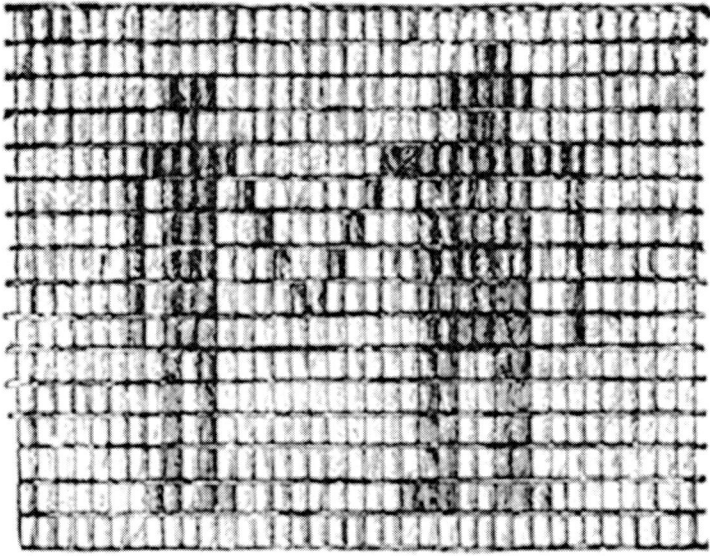

*Section of Wampum Belt Presented to Wm.
Penn—Emblem of Brotherly Love.*

Indian Decorated Bowls.

XI. - HIAWATHA'S WEDDING-FEAST.

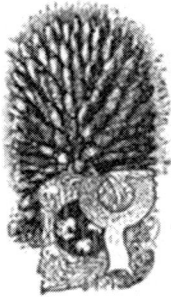

You shall hear how Pau-Puk-Keewis,
How the handsome Yenadizze
Danced at Hiawatha's wedding;
How the gentle Chibiabos,
5   He the sweetest of musicians,
Sang his songs of love and longing;
How Iagoo, the great boaster,
He the marvellous story-teller,
Told his tales of strange adventure,
10   That the feast might be more joyous,
That the time might pass more gayly,
And the guests be more contented.
Sumptuous was the feast Nokomis
Made at Hiawatha's wedding;
15   All the bowls were made of bass-wood,
White and polished very smoothly,
All the spoons of horn of bison,
Black and polished very smoothly.
        She had sent through all the village
20   Messengers with wands of willow,
As a sign of invitation,
As a token of the feasting;
And the wedding guests assembled,
Clad in all their richest raiment,
25   Robes of fur and belts of wampum,
Splendid with their paint and plumage,
Beautiful with beads and tassels.

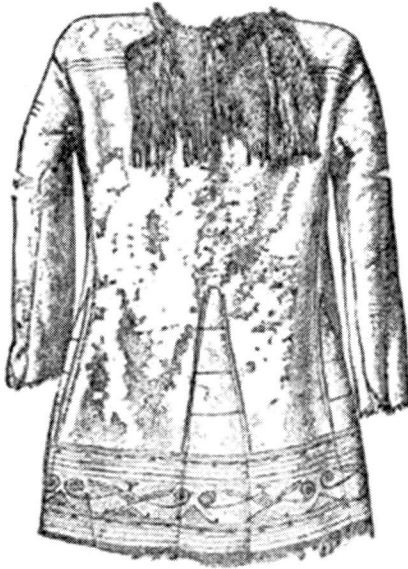

Buckskin Shirt, Embroidered with Wampum.

First they ate the sturgeon, Nahma,

And the pike, the Maskenozha,
30   Caught and cooked by old Nokomis;

Gathering Wild Rice.

Then on pemican they feasted,
Pemican and buffalo marrow,
Haunch of deer and hump of bison,
Yellow cakes of the Mondamin,
35   And the wild rice of the river.
        But the gracious Hiawatha,
And the lovely Laughing Water,
And the careful old Nokomis,
Tasted not the food before them,
40   Only waited on the others,
Only served their guests in silence.
        And when all the guests had finished,
Old Nokomis, brisk and busy,
From an ample pouch of otter,
45   Filled the red stone pipes for smoking
With tobacco from the South-land,
Mixed with bark of the red willow,
And with herbs and leaves of fragrance.
        Then she said, "O Pau-Puk-Keewis,

50 Dance for us your merry dances,
Dance the Beggar's Dance to please us,
That the feast may be more joyous,
That the time may pass more gayly,
And our guests be more contented!"
55 Then the handsome Pau-Puk-Keewis,
He the idle Yenadizze,
He the merry mischief-maker,
Whom the people called the Storm-Fool,
Rose among the guests assembled.
60 Skilled was he in sports and pastimes,
In the merry dance of snow-shoes,
In the play of quoits and ball-play;
Skilled was he in games of hazard,
In all games of skill and hazard,
65 Pugasaing, the Bowl and Counters,
Kuntassoo, the Game of Plum-stones,
Though the warriors called him Faint-heart,
Called him coward, Shaugodaya,
Idler, gambler, Yenadizze,
70 Little heeded he their jesting,
Little cared he for their insults,
For the women and the maidens
Loved the handsome Pau-Puk-Keewis.
He was dressed in shirt of doe-skin,
75 White and soft, and fringed with ermine,
All inwrought with beads of wampum;
He was dressed in deer-skin leggings,
Fringed with hedgehog quills and ermine,
And in moccasins of buck-skin,
80 Thick with quills and beads embroidered.
On his head were plumes of swan's down,
On his heels were tails of foxes,
In one hand a fan of feathers,
And a pipe was in the other.
85 Barred with streaks of red and yellow,
Streaks of blue and bright vermilion,
Shone the face of Pau-Puk-Keewis.
From his forehead fell his tresses,
Smooth, and parted like a woman's,
90 Shining bright with oil, and plaited,

Hung with braids of scented grasses,
As among the guests assembled,
To the sound of flutes and singing,
To the sound of drums and voices,
95   Rose the handsome Pau-Puk-Keewis,
And began his mystic dances.
    First he danced a solemn measure,
Very slow in step and gesture,
In and out among the pine-trees,
100   Through the shadows and the sunshine,
Treading softly like a panther.
Then more swiftly and still swifter,
Whirling, spinning round in circles,
Leaping o'er the guests assembled,
105   Eddying round and round the wigwam,
Till the leaves went whirling with him,
Till the dust and wind together
Swept in eddies round about him.
    Then along the sandy margin
110   Of the lake, the Big-Sea-Water,
On he sped with frenzied gestures,
Stamped upon the sand, and tossed it
Wildly in the air around him;
Till the wind became a whirlwind,
115   Till the sand was blown and sifted
Like great snowdrifts o'er the landscape,
Heaping all the shores with Sand Dunes,
Sand Hills of the Nagow Wudjoo!
    Thus the merry Pau-Puk-Keewis
120   Danced his Beggar's Dance to please them,
And, returning, sat down laughing
There among the guests assembled,
Sat and fanned himself serenely
With his fan of turkey-feathers.
125   Then they said to Chibiabos,
To the friend of Hiawatha,
To the sweetest of all singers,
To the best of all musicians,
"Sing to us, O Chibiabos!
130   Songs of love and songs of longing,
That the feast may be more joyous,

That the time may pass more gayly,
And our guests be more contented!"
And the gentle Chibiabos
135   Sang in accents sweet and tender,
Sang in tones of deep emotion,
Songs of love and songs of longing;
Looking still at Hiawatha,
Looking at fair Laughing Water,
140   Sang he softly, sang in this wise:
"Onaway! Awake, beloved!
Thou the wild-flower of the forest!
Thou the wild-bird of the prairie!
Thou with eyes so soft and fawn-like!
145   "If thou only lookest at me,
I am happy, I am happy,
As the lilies of the prairie,
When they feel the dew upon them!
"Sweet thy breath is as the fragrance
150   Of the wild-flowers in the morning,
As their fragrance is at evening,
In the Moon when leaves are falling.
"Does not all the blood within me
Leap to meet thee, leap to meet thee,
155   As the springs to meet the sunshine,
In the Moon when nights are brightest?
"Onaway! my heart sings to thee,
Sings with joy when thou art near me,
As the sighing, singing branches
160   In the pleasant Moon of Strawberries!
"When thou art not pleased, beloved,
Then my heart is sad and darkened,
As the shining river darkens
When the clouds drop shadows on it!
165   "When thou smilest, my beloved,
Then my troubled heart is brightened,
As in sunshine gleam the ripples
That the cold wind makes in rivers.
"Smiles the earth, and smile the waters,
170   Smile the cloudless skies above us,
But I lose the way of smiling
When thou art no longer near me!

"I myself, myself! behold me!
Blood of my beating heart, behold me!
175   O awake, awake, beloved!
Onaway! awake, beloved!"
    Thus the gentle Chibiabos
Sang his song of love and longing;
And Iagoo, the great boaster,
180   He the marvellous story-teller,
He the friend of old Nokomis,
Jealous of the sweet musician,
Jealous of the applause they gave him,
Saw in all the eyes around him,
185   Saw in all their looks and gestures,
That the wedding guests assembled
Longed to hear his pleasant stories,
His immeasurable falsehoods.
    Very boastful was Iagoo;
190   Never heard he an adventure
But himself had met a greater;
Never any deed of daring
But himself had done a bolder;
Never any marvellous story
195   But himself could tell a stranger.
    Would you listen to his boasting,
Would you only give him credence,
No one ever shot an arrow
Half so far and high as he had;
200   Ever caught so many fishes,
Ever killed so many reindeer,
Ever trapped so many beaver!
    None could run so fast as he could,
None could dive so deep as he could,
205   None could swim so far as he could;
None had made so many journeys,
None had seen so many wonders,
As this wonderful Iagoo,
As this marvellous story-teller!
210   Thus his name became a by-word
And a jest among the people;
And whene'er a boastful hunter
Praised his own address too highly,

Or a warrior, home returning,
215 Talked too much of his achievements,
All his hearers cried, "Iagoo!
Here's Iagoo come among us!"
       He it was who carved the cradle
Of the little Hiawatha,
220 Carved its framework out of linden,
Bound it strong with reindeer sinews;
He it was who taught him later
How to make his bows and arrows,
How to make the bows of ash-tree,
225 And the arrows of the oak-tree.
So among the guests assembled
At my Hiawatha's wedding
Sat Iagoo, old and ugly,
Sat the marvellous story-teller.
230   And they said, "O good Iagoo,
Tell us now a tale of wonder,
Tell us of some strange adventure,
That the feast may be more joyous,
That the time may pass more gayly,
235 And our guests be more contented!"
       And Iagoo answered straightway,
"You shall hear a tale of wonder,
You shall hear the strange adventures
Of Osseo, the Magician,
240 From the Evening Star descended."

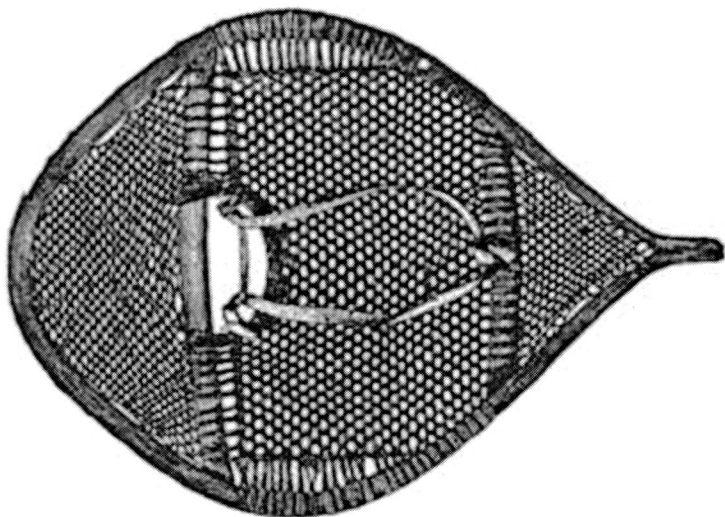

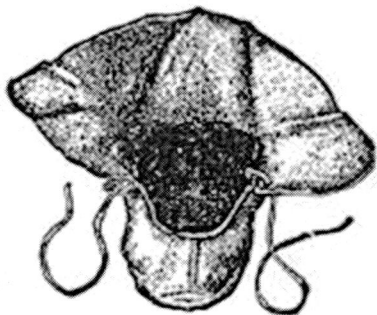

Iroquois Moccasins of Buckskin.

XII. - THE SON OF THE EVENING STAR.

Can it be the sun descending
O'er the level plain of water?
Or the Red Swan floating, flying,
Wounded by the magic arrow,
5 Staining all the waves with crimson,
With the crimson of its life-blood,
Filling all the air with splendor,
With the splendor of its plumage?
Yes; it is the sun descending,
10 Sinking down into the water;
All the sky is stained with purple,
All the water flushed with crimson!
No; it is the Red Swan floating,
Diving down beneath the water;
15 To the sky its wings are lifted,
With its blood the waves are reddened!
Over it the Star of Evening
Melts and trembles through the purple,
Hangs suspended in the twilight.
20 No; it is a bead of wampum
On the robes of the Great Spirit,
As he passes through the twilight,
Walks in silence through the heavens.
This with joy beheld Iagoo
25 And he said in haste: "Behold it!
See the sacred Star of Evening!
You shall hear a tale of wonder,
Hear the story of Osseo!
Son of the Evening Star, Osseo!

30   "Once, in days no more remembered,
Ages nearer the beginning,
When the heavens were closer to us,
And the Gods were more familiar,
In the North-land lived a hunter,
35 With ten young and comely daughters,
Tall and lithe as wands of willow;
Only Oweenee, the youngest,
She the wilful and the wayward,
She the silent dreamy maiden,
40 Was the fairest of the sisters.
        "All these women married warriors,
Married brave and haughty husbands;
Only Oweenee, the youngest,
Laughed and flouted all her lovers,
45 All her young and handsome suitors,
And then married old Osseo,
Old Osseo, poor and ugly,
Broken with age and weak with coughing,
Always coughing like a squirrel.
50   "Ah, but beautiful within him
Was the spirit of Osseo,
From the Evening Star descended,
Star of Evening, Star of Woman,
Star of tenderness and passion!
55 All its fire was in his bosom
All its beauty in his spirit,
All its mystery in his being,
All its splendor in his language!
        "And her lovers, the rejected,
60 Handsome men with belts of wampum,
Handsome men with paint and feathers,
Pointed at her in derision,
Followed her with jest and laughter.
But she said: 'I care not for you,
65 Care not for your belts of wampum,
Care not for your paint and feathers,
Care not for your jest and laughter;
I am happy with Osseo!'
        "Once to some great feast invited,
70 Through the damp and dusk of evening

Walked together the ten sisters,
Walked together with their husbands;
Slowly followed old Osseo,
With fair Oweenee beside him;
75   All the others chatted gayly,
These two only walked in silence.
          "At the western sky Osseo
Gazed intent, as if imploring,
Often stopped and gazed imploring
80   At the trembling Star of Evening,
At the tender Star of Woman;
And they heard him murmur softly,
'Ah, showain nemeshin, Nosa!
Pity, pity me, my father!'
85   "'Listen!' said the elder sister,
'He is praying to his father!
What a pity that the old man
Does not stumble in the pathway,
Does not break his neck by falling!'
90   And they laughed till all the forest
Rang with their unseemly laughter.
          "On their pathway through the woodlands
Lay an oak, by storms uprooted,
Lay the great trunk of an oak-tree,
95   Buried half in leaves and mosses,
Mouldering, crumbling, huge and hollow.
And Osseo, when he saw it,
Gave a shout, a cry of anguish,
Leaped into its yawning cavern,
100 At one end went in an old man,
Wasted, wrinkled, old, and ugly;
From the other came a young man,
Tall and straight and strong and handsome.
          "Thus Osseo was transfigured,
105 Thus restored to youth and beauty;
But, alas for good Osseo,
And for Oweenee, the faithful!
Strangely, too, was she transfigured.
Changed into a weak old woman,
110 With a staff she tottered onward,
Wasted, wrinkled, old, and ugly!

And the sisters and their husbands
Laughed until the echoing forest
Rang with their unseemly laughter.
115   "But Osseo turned not from her,
Walked with slower step beside her,
Took her hand, as brown and withered
As an oak-leaf is in winter,
Called her sweetheart, Nenemoosha,
120 Soothed her with soft words of kindness,
Till they reached the lodge of feasting,
Till they sat down in the wigwam,
Sacred to the Star of Evening,
To the tender Star of Woman.
125   "Wrapt in visions, lost in dreaming,
At the banquet sat Osseo;
All were merry, all were happy,
All were joyous but Osseo.
Neither food nor drink he tasted,
130 Neither did he speak nor listen,
But as one bewildered sat he,
Looking dreamily and sadly,
First at Oweenee, then upward
At the gleaming sky above them.
135   "Then a voice was heard, a whisper,
Coming from the starry distance,
Coming from the empty vastness,
Low, and musical, and tender;
And the voice said: 'O Osseo!
140 O my son, my best beloved!
Broken are the spells that bound you,
All the charms of the magicians,
All the magic powers of evil;
Come to me; ascend, Osseo!
145   "'Taste the food that stands before you:
It is blessed and enchanted,
It has magic virtues in it,
It will change you to a spirit.
All your bowls and all your kettles
150 Shall be wood and clay no longer;
But the bowls be changed to wampum,
And the kettles shall be silver;

They shall shine like shells of scarlet,
Like the fire shall gleam and glimmer.
155   "'And the women shall no longer
Bear the dreary doom of labor,
But be changed to birds, and glisten
With the beauty of the starlight,
Painted with the dusky splendors
160 Of the skies and clouds of evening!'
       "What Osseo heard as whispers,
What as words he comprehended,
Was but music to the others,
Music as of birds afar off,
165 Of the whippoorwill afar off,
Of the lonely Wawonaissa
Singing in the darksome forest.
       "Then the lodge began to tremble,
Straight began to shake and tremble,
170 And they felt it rising, rising,
Slowly through the air ascending,
From the darkness of the tree-tops
Forth into the dewy starlight,
Till it passed the topmost branches;
175 And behold! the wooden dishes
All were changed to shells of scarlet!
And behold! the earthen kettles
All were changed to bowls of silver!
And the roof-poles of the wigwam
180 Were as glittering rods of silver,
And the roof of bark upon them
As the shining shards of beetles.
       "Then Osseo gazed around him,
And he saw the nine fair sisters,
185 All the sisters and their husbands,
Changed to birds of various plumage.
Some were jays and some were magpies,
Others thrushes, others blackbirds;
And they hopped, and sang, and twittered,
190 Perked and fluttered all their feathers,
Strutted in their shining plumage,
And their tails like fans unfolded.
       "Only Oweenee, the youngest,

Was not changed, but sat in silence,
195   Wasted, wrinkled, old, and ugly,
Looking sadly at the others;
Till Osseo, gazing upward,
Gave another cry of anguish,
Such a cry as he had uttered
200   By the oak-tree in the forest.
      "Then returned her youth and beauty,
And her soiled and tattered garments
Were transformed to robes of ermine,
And her staff became a feather,
205   Yes, a shining silver feather!
      "And again the wigwam trembled,
Swayed and rushed through airy currents,
Through transparent cloud and vapor,
And amid celestial splendors
210   On the Evening Star alighted,
As a snow-flake falls on snow-flake,
As a leaf drops on a river,
As the thistle-down on water.
      "Forth with cheerful words of welcome
215   Came the father of Osseo,
He with radiant locks of silver,
He with eyes serene and tender.
And he said: 'My son, Osseo,
Hang the cage of birds you bring there,
220   Hang the cage with rods of silver,
And the birds with glistening feathers,
At the doorway of my wigwam.'
      "At the door he hung the bird-cage,
And they entered in and gladly
225   Listened to Osseo's father,
Ruler of the Star of Evening,
As he said: 'O my Osseo!
I have had compassion on you,
Given you back your youth and beauty,
230   Into birds of various plumage
Changed your sisters and their husbands;
Changed them thus because they mocked you;
In the figure of the old man,
In that aspect sad and wrinkled,

235 Could not see your heart of passion,
 Could not see your youth immortal;
 Only Oweenee, the faithful,
 Saw your naked heart and loved you.
  "'In the lodge that glimmers yonder,
240 In the little star that twinkles
 Through the vapors, on the left hand,
 Lives the envious Evil Spirit,
 The Wabeno, the magician,
 Who transformed you to an old man.
245 Take heed lest his beams fall on you,
 For the rays he darts around him
 Are the power of his enchantment,
 Are the arrows that he uses.'
  "Many years, in peace and quiet,
250 On the peaceful Star of Evening
 Dwelt Osseo with his father;
 Many years, in song and flutter,
 At the doorway of the wigwam,
 Hung the cage with rods of silver,
255 And fair Oweenee, the faithful,
 Bore a son unto Osseo,
 With the beauty of his mother,
 With the courage of his father.
  "And the boy grew up and prospered,
260 And Osseo, to delight him,
 Made him little bows and arrows,
 Opened the great cage of silver,
 And let loose his aunts and uncles,
 All those birds with glossy feathers,
265 For his little son to shoot at.
  "Round and round they wheeled and darted,
 Filled the Evening Star with music,
 With their songs of joy and freedom;
 Filled the Evening Star with splendor,
270 With the fluttering of their plumage;
 Till the boy, the little hunter,
 Bent his bow and shot an arrow,
 Shot a swift and fatal arrow,
 And a bird, with shining feathers,
275 At his feet fell wounded sorely.

       "But, O wondrous transformation!
'T was no bird he saw before him!
'T was a beautiful young woman,
With the arrow in her bosom!
280   "When her blood fell on the planet,
On the sacred Star of Evening,
Broken was the spell of magic,
Powerless was the strange enchantment,
And the youth, the fearless bowman,
285   Suddenly felt himself descending,
Held by unseen hands, but sinking
Downward through the empty spaces,
Downward through the clouds and vapors,
Till he rested on an island,
290   On an island, green and grassy,
Yonder in the Big-Sea-Water.
       "After him he saw descending
All the birds with shining feathers,
Fluttering, falling, wafted downward,
295   Like the painted leaves of Autumn;
And the lodge with poles of silver,
With its roof like wings of beetles,
Like the shining shards of beetles,
By the winds of heaven uplifted,
300   Slowly sank upon the island,
Bringing back the good Osseo,
Bringing Oweenee, the faithful.
       "Then the birds, again transfigured,
Reassumed the shape of mortals,
305   Took their shape, but not their stature;
They remained as Little People,
Like the pygmies, the Puk-Wudjies,
And on pleasant nights of Summer,
When the Evening Star was shining,
310   Hand in hand they danced together
On the island's craggy headlands,
On the sand-beach low and level.
       "Still their glittering lodge is seen there,
On the tranquil Summer evenings,
315   And upon the shore the fisher
Sometimes hears their happy voices,

Sees them dancing in the starlight!"
　　When the story was completed,
When the wondrous tale was ended,
320　Looking round upon his listeners,
Solemnly Iagoo added:
"There are great men, I have known such,
Whom their people understand not,
Whom they even make a jest of,
325　Scoff and jeer at in derision.
From the story of Osseo
Let them learn the fate of jesters!"
　　All the wedding guests delighted
Listened to the marvellous story,
330　Listened laughing and applauding,
And they whispered to each other:
"Does he mean himself, I wonder?
And are we the aunts and uncles?"
　　Then again sang Chibiabos,

The moon was up. One general smile
Was resting on the Indian isle— * *
Rose, mellow'd through the silver gleam,
Soft as the landscape of a dream.

335   Sang a song of love and longing,
In those accents sweet and tender,
In those tones of pensive sadness,
Sang a maiden's lamentation
For her lover, her Algonquin.
340   "When I think of my beloved,
Ah me! think of my beloved,
When my heart is thinking of him,
O my sweetheart, my Algonquin!
         "Ah, me! when I parted from him,
345   Round my neck he hung the wampum,
As a pledge, the snow-white wampum,
O my sweetheart, my Algonquin!
         "I will go with you, he whispered,
Ah me! to your native country;
350   Let me go with you, he whispered,
O my sweetheart, my Algonquin!
         "Far away, away, I answered,
Very far away, I answered,
Ah me! is my native country,
355   O my sweetheart, my Algonquin!
         "When I looked back to behold him,
Where we parted, to behold him,
After me he still was gazing,
O my sweetheart, my Algonquin!
360   "By the tree he still was standing,
By the fallen tree was standing,
That had dropped into the water,
O my sweetheart, my Algonquin!
         "When I think of my beloved,
365   Ah me! think of my beloved,
When my heart is thinking of him,
O my sweetheart, my Algonquin!"
         Such was Hiawatha's Wedding,
Such the dance of Pau-Puk-Keewis,
370   Such the story of Iagoo,
Such the songs of Chibiabos;
Thus the wedding banquet ended,
And the wedding guests departed,
Leaving Hiawatha happy
375   With the night and Minnehaha.

Apache Indians Lassoing Wild Horses.

XIII. - BLESSING THE CORN-FIELDS

Sing, O song of Hiawatha,
Of the happy days that followed,
In the land of the Ojibways,
In the pleasant land and peaceful!
5 Sing the mysteries of Mondamin,
Sing the Blessing of the Corn-fields!
Buried was the bloody hatchet,
Buried was the dreadful war-club,
Buried were all warlike weapons,
10 And the war-cry was forgotten.
There was peace among the nations;
Unmolested roved the hunters,
Built the birch canoe for sailing,
Caught the fish in lake and river,
15 Shot the deer and trapped the beaver;
Unmolested worked the women,
Made their sugar from the maple,
Gathered wild rice in the meadows,
Dressed the skins of deer and beaver.
20 All around the happy village
Stood the maize-fields, green and shining,
Waved the green plumes of Mondamin,
Waved his soft and sunny tresses
Filling all the land with plenty.
25 'T was the women who in Spring-time
Planted the broad fields and fruitful,
Buried in the earth Mondamin;
'T was the women who in Autumn
Stripped the yellow husks of harvest,

30   Stripped the garments from Mondamin,
         Even as Hiawatha taught them.
                Once, when all the maize was planted,
         Hiawatha, wise and thoughtful,
         Spake and said to Minnehaha,
35   To his wife, the Laughing Water:
         "You shall bless to-night the corn-fields,
         Draw a magic circle round them,
         To protect them from destruction,
         Blast of mildew, blight of insect,
40   Wagemin, the thief of corn-fields,
         Paimosaid, who steals the maize-ear!
              "In the night, when all is silence,
         In the night, when all is darkness,
         When the Spirit of Sleep, Nepahwin,
45   Shuts the doors of all the wigwams,
         So that not an ear can hear you,
         So that not an eye can see you,
         Rise up from your bed in silence,
         Lay aside your garments wholly,
50   Walk around the fields you planted,
         Round the borders of the corn-fields,
         Covered by your tresses only,
         Robed with darkness as a garment.
              "Thus the fields shall be more fruitful,
55   And the passing of your footsteps
         Draw a magic circle round them,
         So that neither blight nor mildew,
         Neither burrowing worm nor insect,
         Shall pass o'er the magic circle;
60   Not the dragon-fly, Kwo-ne-she,
         Nor the spider, Subbekashe,
         Nor the grasshopper, Pah-puk-keena,
         Nor the mighty caterpillar,
         Way-muk-kwana, with the bear-skin,
65   King of all the caterpillars!"
              On the tree-tops near the corn-fields
         Sat the hungry crows and ravens,
         Kahgahgee, the King of Ravens,
         With his band of black marauders,
70   And they laughed at Hiawatha,

Till the tree-tops shook with laughter,
With their melancholy laughter
At the words of Hiawatha.
"Hear him!" said they; "hear the Wise Man,
75   Hear the plots of Hiawatha!"
      When the noiseless night descended
Broad and dark o'er field and forest,
When the mournful Wawonaissa
Sorrowing sang among the hemlocks,
80   And the Spirit of Sleep, Nepahwin,
Shut the doors of all the wigwams,
From her bed rose Laughing Water,
Laid aside her garments wholly,
And with darkness clothed and guarded,
85   Unashamed and unaffrighted,
Walked securely round the corn-fields,
Drew the sacred, magic circle
Of her footprints round the corn-fields.
      No one but the Midnight only
90   Saw her beauty in the darkness,
No one but the Wawonaissa
Heard the panting of her bosom;
Guskewau, the darkness, wrapped her
Closely in his sacred mantle,
95   So that none might see her beauty,
So that none might boast, "I saw her!"
      On the morrow, as the day dawned,
Kahgahgee, the King of Ravens,
Gathered all his black marauders,
100   Crows and blackbirds, jays and ravens,
Clamorous on the dusky tree-tops,
And descended, fast and fearless,
On the fields of Hiawatha,
On the grave of the Mondamin.
105   "We will drag Mondamin," said they,
"From the grave where he is buried,
Spite of all the magic circles
Laughing Water draws around it,
Spite of all the sacred footprints
110   Minnehaha stamps upon it!"
      But the wary Hiawatha,

Ever thoughtful, careful, watchful,
Had o'erheard the scornful laughter
When they mocked him from the tree-tops.
115 "Kaw!" he said, "my friends the ravens!
Kahgahgee, my King of Ravens!
I will teach you all a lesson
That shall not be soon forgotten!"
      He had risen before the daybreak,
120 He had spread o'er all the corn-fields
Snares to catch the black marauders,
And was lying now in ambush
in the neighboring grove of pine-trees,
Waiting for the crows and blackbirds,
125 Waiting for the jays and ravens.
      Soon they came with caw and clamor,
Rush of wings and cry of voices,
To their work of devastation,
Settling down upon the corn-fields,
130 Delving deep with beak and talon,
For the body of Mondamin.
And with all their craft and cunning,
All their skill in wiles of warfare,
They perceived no danger near them,
135 Till their claws became entangled,
Till they found themselves imprisoned
In the snares of Hiawatha.
      From his place of ambush came he,
Striding terrible among them,
140 And so awful was his aspect
That the bravest quailed with terror.
Without mercy he destroyed them
Right and left, by tens and twenties,
And their wretched, lifeless bodies
145 Hung aloft on poles for scarecrows
Round the consecrated corn-fields,
As a signal of his vengeance,
As a warning to marauders.
      Only Kahgahgee, the leader,
150 Kahgahgee, the King of Ravens,
He alone was spared among them
As a hostage for his people.

With his prisoner-string he bound him,
Led him captive to his wigwam,
155 Tied him fast with cords of elm-bark
To the ridge-pole of his wigwam.
   "Kahgahgee, my raven!" said he,
"You the leader of the robbers,
You the plotter of this mischief,
160 The contriver of this outrage,
I will keep you, I will hold you,
As a hostage for your people,
As a pledge of good behavior!"
   And he left him, grim and sulky,
165 Sitting in the morning sunshine
On the summit of the wigwam,
Croaking fiercely his displeasure,
Flapping his great sable pinions,
Vainly struggling for his freedom,
170 Vainly calling on his people!
   Summer passed, and Shawondasee
Breathed his sighs o'er all the landscape,
From the South-land sent his ardors,
Wafted kisses warm and tender;
175 And the maize-field grew and ripened,
Till it stood in all the splendor
Of its garments green and yellow,
Of its tassels and its plumage,
And the maize-ears full and shining
180 Gleamed from bursting sheaths of verdure.
   Then Nokomis, the old woman,
Spake, and said to Minnehaha:
"'T is the Moon when leaves are falling;
All the wild-rice has been gathered,
185 And the maize is ripe and ready;
Let us gather in the harvest,
Let us wrestle with Mondamin,
Strip him of his plumes and tassels,
Of his garments green and yellow!"
190   And the merry Laughing Water
Went rejoicing from the wigwam,
With Nokomis, old and wrinkled,
And they called the women round them,

Called the young men and the maidens,
195   To the harvest of the corn-fields,

To the husking of the maize-ear.
        On the border of the forest,
Underneath the fragrant pine-trees,
Sat the old men and the warriors
200   Smoking in the pleasant shadow.
In uninterrupted silence
Looked they at the gamesome labor
Of the young men and the women;
Listened to their noisy talking,
205   To their laughter and their singing,
Heard them chattering like the magpies,
Heard them laughing like the blue-jays,
Heard them singing like the robins.
        And whene'er some lucky maiden
210   Found a red ear in the husking,
Found a maize-ear red as blood is,
"Nushka!" cried they all together,

"Nushka! you shall have a sweetheart,
You shall have a handsome husband!"
215 "Ugh!" the old men all responded,
From their seats beneath the pine-trees.
  And whene'er a youth or maiden
Found a crooked ear in husking,
Found a maize-ear in the husking
220 Blighted, mildewed, or misshapen,
Then they laughed and sang together,
Crept and limped about the corn-fields,
Mimicked in their gait and gestures
Some old man, bent almost double,
225 Singing singly or together:
"Wagemin, the thief of corn-fields!
Paimosaid, the skulking robber!"
  Till the corn-fields rang with laughter,
Till from Hiawatha's wigwam
230 Kahgahgee, the King of Ravens,
Screamed and quivered in his anger,
And from all the neighboring tree-tops
Cawed and croaked the black marauders.
"Ugh!" the old men all responded,
235 From their seats beneath the pine-trees!

XIV. - PICTURE-WRITING.

In those days said Hiawatha,
"Lo! how all things fade and perish!
From the memory of the old men
Pass away the great traditions,
The achievements of the warriors,
The adventures of the hunters,
All the wisdom of the Medas,
All the craft of the Wabenos,
All the marvellous dreams and visions
Of the Jossakeeds, the Prophets!
        "Great men die and are forgotten,
Wise men speak; their words of wisdom
Perish in the ears that hear them,
Do not reach the generations
That, as yet unborn, are waiting
In the great, mysterious darkness
Of the speechless days that shall be!
        "On the grave-posts of our fathers
Are no signs, no figures painted;
Who are in those graves we know not,
Only know they are our fathers.
Of what kith they are and kindred,
From what old, ancestral Totem,
Be it Eagle, Bear or Beaver,
They descended, this we know not,
Only know they are our fathers.
        "Face to face we speak together,
But we cannot speak when absent,
Cannot send our voices from us

30 To the friends that dwell afar off;
Cannot send a secret message,
But the bearer learns our secret,
May pervert it, may betray it,
May reveal it unto others."
35   Thus said Hiawatha, walking
In the solitary forest,
Pondering, musing in the forest,
On the welfare of his people.
   From his pouch he took his colors,
40 Took his paints of different colors,
On the smooth bark of a birch-tree
Painted many shapes and figures,
Wonderful and mystic figures,
And each figure had a meaning,
45 Each some word or thought suggested.
   Gitche Manito the Mighty,
He, the Master of Life, was painted
As an egg, with points projecting
To the four winds of the heavens.
50 Everywhere is the Great Spirit,
Was the meaning of this symbol.
   Mitche Manito the Mighty,
He the dreadful Spirit of Evil,
As a serpent was depicted,
55 As Kenabeek, the great serpent.
Very crafty, very cunning,
Is the creeping Spirit of Evil,
Was the meaning of this symbol.
   Life and Death he drew as circles,
60 Life was white, but Death was darkened;
Sun and moon and stars he painted,
Man and beast, and fish and reptile,
Forests, mountains, lakes, and rivers.
   For the earth he drew a straight line,
65 For the sky a bow above it;
White the space between for day-time,
Filled with little stars for night-time;
On the left a point for sunrise,
On the right a point for sunset,
70 On the top a point for noontide,

And for rain and cloudy weather
Waving lines descending from it.
       Footprints pointing towards a wigwam
Were a sign of invitation,
75   Were a sign of guests assembling;
Bloody hands with palms uplifted
Were a symbol of destruction,
Were a hostile sign and symbol.
       All these things did Hiawatha
80   Show unto his wondering people,
And interpreted their meaning,
And he said: "Behold, your grave-posts
Have no mark, no sign, nor symbol.
Go and paint them all with figures;
85   Each one with its household symbol,
With its own ancestral Totem;
So that those who follow after
May distinguish them and know them."
       And they painted on the grave-posts
90   On the graves yet unforgotten,
Each his own ancestral Totem,
Each the symbol of his household;
Figures of the Bear and Reindeer,
Of the Turtle, Crane, and Beaver,
95   Each inverted as a token
That the owner was departed,
That the chief who bore the symbol
Lay beneath in dust and ashes.
       And the Jossakeeds, the Prophets,
100   The Wabenos, the Magicians,
And the Medicine-men, the Medas,
Painted upon bark and deer-skin
Figures for the songs they chanted,
For each song a separate symbol,
105   Figures mystical and awful,
Figures strange and brightly colored;
And each figure had its meaning,
Each some magic song suggested.
       The Great Spirit, the Creator,
110   Flashing light through all the heaven;
The Great Serpent, the Kenabeek,

With his bloody crest erected,
Creeping, looking into heaven;
In the sky the sun, that glistens,
115   And the moon eclipsed and dying;
Owl and eagle, crane and hen-hawk,
And the cormorant, bird of magic;
Headless men, that walk the heavens,
Bodies lying pierced with arrows,
120   Bloody hands of death uplifted,
Flags on graves, and great war-captains
Grasping both the earth and heaven!
      Such as these the shapes they painted
On the birch-bark and the deer-skin;
125   Songs of war and songs of hunting,
Songs of medicine and of magic,
All were written in these figures,
For each figure had its meaning,
Each its separate song recorded.
130   Nor forgotten was the Love-Song,
The most subtle of all medicines,
The most potent spell of magic,
Dangerous more than war or hunting!
Thus the Love-Song was recorded,
135   Symbol and interpretation.
      First a human figure standing,
Painted in the brightest scarlet;
'T is the lover, the musician,
And the meaning is, "My painting
140   Makes me powerful over others."
      Then the figure seated, singing,
Playing on a drum of magic,
And the interpretation, "Listen!
'T is my voice you hear, my singing!"
145   Then the same red figure seated
In the shelter of a wigwam,
And the meaning of the symbol,
"I will come and sit beside you
In the mystery of my passion!"
150   Then two figures, man and woman,
Standing hand in hand together
With their hands so clasped together

That they seem in one united,
And the words thus represented
155 Are, "I see your heart within you,
And your cheeks are red with blushes!"
Next the maiden on an island,
In the centre of an island;
And the song this shape suggested
160 Was, "Though you were at a distance,
Were upon some far-off island,
Such the spell I cast upon you,
Such the magic power of passion,
I could straightway draw you to me!"
165 Then the figure of the maiden
Sleeping, and the lover near her,
Whispering to her in her slumbers,
Saying, "Though you were far from me
In the land of Sleep and Silence,
170 Still the voice of love would reach you!"
And the last of all the figures
Was a heart within a circle,
Drawn within a magic circle;
And the image had this meaning:
175 "Naked lies your heart before me,
To your naked heart I whisper!"
Thus it was that Hiawatha,
In his wisdom, taught the people
All the mysteries of painting,
180 All the art of Picture-Writing,
On the smooth bark of the birch-tree,
On the white skin of the reindeer,
On the grave-posts of the village.

"Danced the medicine-dance around him;
And upstarting wild and haggard."

XV. - HIAWATHA'S LAMENTATION.

In those days the Evil Spirits,
All the Manitos of mischief,
Fearing Hiawatha's wisdom,
And his love for Chibiabos,
5   Jealous of their faithful friendship,
And their noble words and actions,
Made at length a league against them,
To molest them and destroy them.
    Hiawatha, wise and wary,
10 Often said to Chibiabos,
"O my brother! do not leave me,
Lest the Evil Spirits harm you!"
Chibiabos, young and heedless,
Laughing shook his coal-black tresses,
15 Answered ever sweet and childlike,
"Do not fear for me, O brother!
Harm and evil come not near me!"
        Once when Peboan, the Winter,
Roofed with ice the Big-Sea-Water,
20 When the snow-flakes, whirling downward,
Hissed among the withered oak-leaves,
Changed the pine-trees into wigwams,
Covered all the earth with silence,—
Armed with arrows, shod with snow-shoes,
25 Heeding not his brother's warning,
Fearing not the Evil Spirits,
Forth to hunt the deer with antlers
All alone went Chibiabos.
        Right across the Big-Sea-Water

30 Sprang with speed the deer before him.
  With the wind and snow he followed,
  O'er the treacherous ice he followed,
  Wild with all the fierce commotion
  And the rapture of the hunting.
35   But beneath, the Evil Spirits
  Lay in ambush, waiting for him,
  Broke the treacherous ice beneath him,
  Dragged him downward to the bottom,
  Buried in the sand his body.
40 Unktahee, the god of water,
  He the god of the Dacotahs,
  Drowned him in the deep abysses
  Of the lake of Gitche Gumee.
    From the headlands Hiawatha
45 Sent forth such a wail of anguish,
  Such a fearful lamentation,
  That the bison paused to listen,
  And the wolves howled from the prairies,
  And the thunder in the distance
50 Starting answered "Baim-wawa!"
    Then his face with black he painted,
  With his robe his head he covered,
  In his wigwam sat lamenting,
  Seven long weeks he sat lamenting,
55 Uttering still this moan of sorrow:—
    "He is dead, the sweet musician!
  He the sweetest of all singers!
  He has gone from us forever,
  He has moved a little nearer
60 To the Master of all music,
  To the Master of all singing!
  O my brother, Chibiabos!"
    And the melancholy fir-trees
  Waved their dark green fans above him,
65 Waved their purple cones above him,
  Sighing with him to console him,
  Mingling with his lamentation
  Their complaining, their lamenting.
    Came the Spring, and all the forest
70 Looked in vain for Chibiabos;

Sighed the rivulet, Sebowisha,
Sighed the rushes in the meadow.
    From the tree-tops sang the bluebird,
Sang the bluebird, the Owaissa,
75   "Chibiabos! Chibiabos!
He is dead, the sweet musician!"
    From the wigwam sang the robin,
Sang the Opechee, the robin,
"Chibiabos! Chibiabos!
80   He is dead, the sweetest singer!"
    And at night through all the forest
Went the whippoorwill complaining,
Wailing went the Wawonaissa,
"Chibiabos! Chibiabos!
85   He is dead, the sweet musician!
He the sweetest of all singers!"
    Then the medicine-men, the Medas,
The magicians, the Wabenos,
And the Jossakeeds, the prophets,
90   Came to visit Hiawatha;
Built a Sacred Lodge beside him,
To appease him, to console him,
Walked in silent, grave procession,
Bearing each a pouch of healing,
95   Skin of beaver, lynx, or otter,
Filled with magic roots and simples,
Filled with very potent medicines.
    When he heard their steps approaching,
Hiawatha ceased lamenting,
100   Called no more on Chibiabos;
Naught he questioned, naught he answered,
But his mournful head uncovered,
From his face the mourning colors
Washed he slowly and in silence,
105   Slowly and in silence followed
Onward to the Sacred Wigwam.
    There a magic drink they gave him,
Made of Nahma-wusk, the spearmint,
And Wabeno-wusk, the yarrow,
110   Roots of power, and herbs of healing;
Beat their drums, and shook their rattles;

Chanted singly and in chorus,
Mystic songs, like these, they chanted.
   "I myself, myself! behold me!

   "Then the medicine-men, the Medas,
   The magicians, the Wabenos,
   And the Jossakeeds, the prophets,
   Came to visit Hiawatha."

115   'T is the great Gray Eagle talking;
     Come, ye white crows, come and hear him!
     The loud-speaking thunder helps me;
     All the unseen spirits help me;
     I can hear their voices calling,
120   All around the sky I hear them!
     I can blow you strong, my brother,
     I can heal you, Hiawatha!"
       "Hi-au-ha!" replied the chorus,

"Way-ha-way!" the mystic chorus.
125   "Friends of mine are all the serpents!
Hear me shake my skin of hen-hawk!
Mahng, the white loon, I can kill him;
I can shoot your heart and kill it!
I can blow you strong, my brother,
130 I can heal you, Hiawatha!"
         "Hi-au-ha!" replied the chorus,
"Way-ha-way!" the mystic chorus.
         "I myself, myself! the prophet!
When I speak the wigwam trembles,
135 Shakes the Sacred Lodge with terror,
Hands unseen begin to shake it!
When I walk, the sky I tread on
Bends and makes a noise beneath me!
I can blow you strong, my brother!
140 Rise and speak, O Hiawatha!"
         "Hi-au-ha!" replied the chorus,
"Way-ha-way!" the mystic chorus.
         Then they shook their medicine-pouches
O'er the head of Hiawatha,
145 Danced their medicine-dance around him;
And upstarting wild and haggard,
Like a man from dreams awakened,
He was healed of all his madness.
As the clouds are swept from heaven,
150 Straightway from his brain departed
All his moody melancholy;
As the ice is swept from rivers,
Straightway from his heart departed
All his sorrow and affliction.
155   Then they summoned Chibiabos
From his grave beneath the waters,
From the sands of Gitche Gumee
Summoned Hiawatha's brother.
And so mighty was the magic
160 Of that cry and invocation,
That he heard it as he lay there
Underneath the Big-Sea-Water;
From the sand he rose and listened,
Heard the music and the singing,

165 Came, obedient to the summons,
  To the doorway of the wigwam,
  But to enter they forbade him.
   Through a chink a coal they gave him,
  Through the door a burning fire-brand;
170 Ruler in the Land of Spirits,
  Ruler o'er the dead, they made him,
  Telling him a fire to kindle
  For all those that died thereafter,
  Camp-fires for their night encampments
175 On their solitary journey
  To the kingdom of Ponemah,
  To the land of the Hereafter.
   From the village of his childhood,
  From the homes of those who knew him,
180 Passing silent through the forest,
  Like a smoke-wreath wafted sideways,
  Slowly vanished Chibiabos!
  Where he passed, the branches moved not,
  Where he trod, the grasses bent not
185 And the fallen leaves of last year
  Made no sound beneath his footsteps.
   Four whole days he journeyed onward
  Down the pathway of the dead men;
  On the dead man's strawberry feasted,
190 Crossed the melancholy river,
  On the swinging log he crossed it,—
  Came unto the Lake of Silver,
  In the Stone Canoe was carried
  To the Islands of the Blessed,
195 To the land of ghosts and shadows.
   On that journey, moving slowly,
  Many weary spirits saw he,
  Panting under heavy burdens,
  Laden with war-clubs, bows and arrows,
200 Robes of fur, and pots and kettles,
  And with food that friends had given
  For that solitary journey.
   "Ay! why do the living," said they,
  "Lay such heavy burdens on us!
205 Better were it to go naked,

Better were it to go fasting,
Than to bear such heavy burdens
On our long and weary journey!"
  Forth then issued Hiawatha,
210   Wandered eastward, wandered westward,
Teaching men the use of simples
And the antidotes for poisons,
And the cure of all diseases.
Thus was first made known to mortals
215   All the mystery of Medamin,
All the sacred art of healing.

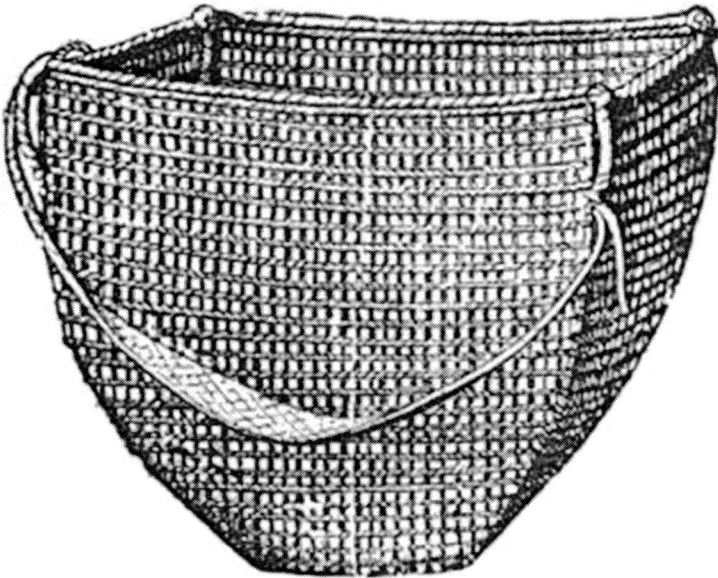

Basket Used by the Pawnee Indians for Carrying
Corn or Berries.

"With the sacred belt of Wampum."

XVI. - PAU-PUK-KEEWIS.

You shall hear how Pau-Puk-Keewis,
He, the handsome Yenadizze,
Whom the people called the Storm Fool,
Vexed the village with disturbance.
5 You shall hear of all his mischief,
And his flight from Hiawatha,
And his wondrous transmigrations,
And the end of his adventures.
On the shores of Gitche Gumee,
10 On the dunes of Nagow Wudjoo,
By the shining Big-Sea-Water
Stood the lodge of Pau-Puk-Keewis.
It was he who in his frenzy
Whirled these drifting sands together,
15 On the dunes of Nagow Wudjoo,
When, among the guests assembled,
He so merrily and madly
Danced at Hiawatha's wedding,
Danced the Beggar's Dance to please them.
20 Now, in search of new adventures,
From his lodge went Pau-Puk-Keewis,
Came with speed into the village,
Found the young men all assembled
In the lodge of old Iagoo,
25 Listening to his monstrous stories,
To his wonderful adventures.
He was telling them the story
Of Ojeeg, the Summer-Maker,
How he made a hole in heaven,

30   How he climbed up into heaven,
    And let out the summer-weather,
    The perpetual, pleasant Summer;
    How the Otter first essayed it;
    How the Beaver, Lynx, and Badger
35   Tried in turn the great achievement,
    From the summit of the mountain
    Smote their fists against the heavens,
    Smote against the sky their foreheads,
    Cracked the sky, but could not break it;
40   How the Wolverine, uprising,
    Made him ready for the encounter,
    Bent his knees down, like a squirrel,
    Drew his arms back, like a cricket.
        "Once he leaped," said old Iagoo,
45   "Once he leaped, and lo! above him
    Bent the sky, as ice in rivers
    When the waters rise beneath it;
    Twice he leaped, and lo! above him
    Cracked the sky, as ice in rivers
50   When the freshet is at highest!
    Thrice he leaped, and lo! above him
    Broke the shattered sky asunder,
    And he disappeared within it,
    And Ojeeg, the Fisher Weasel,
55   With a bound went in behind him!"
        "Hark you!" shouted Pau-Puk-Keewis
    As he entered at the doorway;
    "I am tired of all this talking,
    Tired of old Iagoo's stories,
60   Tired of Hiawatha's wisdom.
    Here is something to amuse you,
    Better than this endless talking."
        Then from out his pouch of wolf-skin
    Forth he drew, with solemn manner,
65   All the game of Bowl and Counters,
    Pugasaing, with thirteen pieces.
    White on one side were they painted,
    And vermilion on the other;
    Two Kenabeeks or great serpents,
70   Two Ininewug or wedge-men,

One great war-club, Pugamaugun,
And one slender fish, the Keego,
Four round pieces, Ozawabeeks,
And three Sheshebwug or ducklings.
75   All were made of bone and painted,
All except the Ozawabeeks;
These were brass, on one side burnished,
And were black upon the other.
        In a wooden bowl he placed them,
80   Shook and jostled them together,
Threw them on the ground before him,
Thus exclaiming and explaining:
"Red side up are all the pieces,
And one great Kenabeek standing
85   On the bright side of a brass piece,
On a burnished Ozawabeek;
Thirteen tens and eight are counted."

Then again he shook the pieces,
Shook and jostled them together,
90   Threw them on the ground before him,
Still exclaiming and explaining:
"White are both the great Kenabeeks,
White the Ininewug, the wedge-men,
Red are all the other pieces;
95   Five tens and an eight are counted."
Thus he taught the game of hazard,
Thus displayed it and explained it,
Running through its various chances,
Various changes, various meanings:
100   Twenty curious eyes stared at him,
Full of eagerness stared at him.
"Many games," said old Iagoo,
"Many games of skill and hazard
Have I seen in different nations,
105   Have I played in different countries.
He who plays with old Iagoo
Must have very nimble fingers;
Though you think yourself so skilful
I can beat you, Pau-Puk-Keewis,
110   I can even give you lessons
In your game of Bowl and Counters!"
So they sat and played together,
All the old men and the young men,
Played for dresses, weapons, wampum,
115   Played till midnight, played till morning,
Played until the Yenadizze,
Till the cunning Pau-Puk-Keewis,
Of their treasures had despoiled them,
Of the best of all their dresses,
120   Shirts of deer-skin, robes of ermine,
Belts of wampum, crests of feathers,
Warlike weapons, pipes and pouches.
Twenty eyes glared wildly at him,
Like the eyes of wolves glared at him.
125   Said the lucky Pau-Puk-Keewis:
"In my wigwam I am lonely,
In my wanderings and adventures
I have need of a companion,

Fain would have a Meshinauwa,
130   An attendant and pipe-bearer.
I will venture all these winnings,
All these garments heaped about me,
All this wampum, all these feathers,
On a single throw will venture
135   All against the young man yonder!"
'T was a youth of sixteen summers,
'T was a nephew of Iagoo;
Face-in-a-Mist, the people called him.
        As the fire burns in a pipe-head
140   Dusky red beneath the ashes,
So beneath his shaggy eyebrows
Glowed the eyes of old Iagoo.
"Ugh!" he answered very fiercely;
"Ugh!" they answered all and each one.
145   Seized the wooden bowl the old man,
Closely in his bony fingers
Clutched the fatal bowl, Onagon,
Shook it fiercely and with fury,
Made the pieces ring together
150   As he threw them down before him.
        Red were both the great Kenabeeks,
Red the Ininewug, the wedge-men,
Red the Sheshebwug, the ducklings,
Black the four brass Ozawabeeks,
155   White alone the fish, the Keego;
Only five the pieces counted!
        Then the smiling Pau-Puk-Keewis
Shook the bowl and threw the pieces;
Lightly in the air he tossed them,
160   And they fell about him scattered;
Dark and bright the Ozawabeeks,
Red and white the other pieces,
And upright among the others
One Ininewug was standing,
165   Even as crafty Pau-Puk-Keewis
Stood alone among the players,
Saying, "Five tens! mine the game is!"
        Twenty eyes glared at him fiercely,
Like the eyes of wolves glared at him,

170   As he turned and left the wigwam,
        Followed by his Meshinauwa,
        By the nephew of Iagoo,
        By the tall and graceful stripling,
        Bearing in his arms the winnings,
175   Shirts of deer-skin, robes of ermine,
        Belts of wampum, pipes and weapons.
            "Carry them," said Pau-Puk-Keewis,
        Pointing with his fan of feathers,
        "To my wigwam far to eastward,
180   On the dunes of Nagow Wudjoo!"
            Hot and red with smoke and gambling
        Were the eyes of Pau-Puk-Keewis
        As he came forth to the freshness
        Of the pleasant Summer morning.
185   All the birds were singing gayly,
        All the streamlets flowing swiftly,
        And the heart of Pau-Puk-Keewis
        Sang with pleasure as the birds sing,
        Beat with triumph like the streamlets,
190   As he wandered through the village,
        In the early gray of morning,
        With his fan of turkey-feathers,
        With his plumes and tufts of swan's down,
        Till he reached the farthest wigwam,
195   Reached the lodge of Hiawatha.
            Silent was it and deserted;
        No one met him at the doorway,
        No one came to bid him welcome;
        But the birds were singing round it,
200   In and out and round the doorway,
        Hopping, singing, fluttering, feeding,
        And aloft upon the ridge-pole
        Kahgahgee, the King of Ravens,
        Sat with fiery eyes, and, screaming,
205   Flapped his wings at Pau-Puk-Keewis.
            "All are gone! the lodge is empty!"
        Thus it was spake Pau-Puk-Keewis,
        In his heart resolving mischief;—
        "Gone is wary Hiawatha,
210   Gone the silly Laughing Water,

Gone Nokomis, the old woman,
And the lodge is left unguarded!"
    By the neck he seized the raven,
Whirled it round him like a rattle,
215   Like a medicine-pouch he shook it,
Strangled Kahgahgee, the raven,
From the ridge-pole of the wigwam
Left its lifeless body hanging,
As an insult to its master,
220   As a taunt to Hiawatha.
    With a stealthy step he entered,
Round the lodge in wild disorder
Threw the household things about him,
Piled together in confusion
225   Bowls of wood and earthen kettles,
Robes of buffalo and beaver,
Skins of otter, lynx, and ermine,
As an insult to Nokomis,
As a taunt to Minnehaha.
230   Then departed Pau-Puk-Keewis,
Whistling, singing through the forest,
Whistling gayly to the squirrels,
Who from hollow boughs above him
Dropped their acorn-shells upon him,
235   Singing gayly to the wood-birds,
Who from out the leafy darkness
Answered with a song as merry.
    Then he climbed the rocky headlands
Looking o'er the Gitche Gumee,
240   Perched himself upon their summit,
Waiting full of mirth and mischief
The return of Hiawatha.
    Stretched upon his back he lay there;
Far below him plashed the waters,
245   Plashed and washed the dreamy waters;
Far above him swam the heavens,
Swam the dizzy, dreamy heavens;
Round him hovered, fluttered, rustled,
Hiawatha's mountain chickens,
250   Flock-wise swept and wheeled about him,
Almost brushed him with their pinions.

And he killed them as he lay there,
Slaughtered them by tens and twenties,
Threw their bodies down the headland,
255   Threw them on the beach below him,
Till at length Kayoshk, the sea-gull,
Perched upon a crag above them,
Shouted: "It is Pau-Puk-Keewis!
He is slaying us by hundreds!
260   Send a message to our brother,
Tidings send to Hiawatha!"

XVII. - THE HUNTING OF PAU-PUK-KEEWIS.

Full of wrath was Hiawatha
When he came into the village,
Found the people in confusion,
Heard of all the misdemeanors,
5   All the malice and the mischief,
Of the cunning Pau-Puk-Keewis.
Hard his breath came through his nostrils,
Through his teeth he buzzed and muttered
Words of anger and resentment,
10   Hot and humming like a hornet.
"I will slay this Pau-Puk-Keewis,
Slay this mischief-maker!" said he.
"Not so long and wide the world is,
Not so rude and rough the way is,
15   That my wrath shall not attain him,
That my vengeance shall not reach him!"
Then in swift pursuit departed
Hiawatha and the hunters
On the trail of Pau-Puk-Keewis,
20   Through the forest, where he passed it,
To the headlands where he rested;
But they found not Pau-Puk-Keewis,
Only in the trampled grasses,
In the whortleberry-bushes,
25   Found the couch where he had rested,
Found the impress of his body.
From the lowlands far beneath them,
From the Muskoday, the meadow,

Pau-Puk-Keewis, turning backward,
30   Made a gesture of defiance,
Made a gesture of derision;
And aloud cried Hiawatha,
From the summit of the mountains:
"Not so long and wide the world is,
35   Not so rude and rough the way is,
But my wrath shall overtake you,
And my vengeance shall attain you!"
     Over rock and over river,
Through the bush, and brake, and forest,
40   Ran the cunning Pau-Puk-Keewis;
Like an antelope he bounded,
Till he came unto a streamlet
In the middle of the forest,
To a streamlet still and tranquil,
45   That had overflowed its margin,
To a dam made by the beavers,
To a pond of quiet water,
Where knee-deep the trees were standing,
Where the water-lilies floated,
50   Where the rushes waved and whispered.
     On the dam stood Pau-Puk-Keewis,
On the dam of trunks and branches,
Through whose chinks the water spouted,
O'er whose summit flowed the streamlet.
55   From the bottom rose the beaver,
Looked with two great eyes of wonder,
Eyes that seemed to ask a question,
At the stranger, Pau-Puk-Keewis.
     On the dam stood Pau-Puk-Keewis,
60   O'er his ankles flowed the streamlet,
Flowed the bright and silvery water,
And he spake unto the beaver,
With a smile he spake in this wise:

"From the bottom rose a beaver,
Looked with two great eyes of wonder,
Eyes that seemed to ask a question."

"O my friend Ahmeek, the beaver,
65   Cool and pleasant is the water;
Let me dive into the water,
Let me rest there in your lodges;
Change me, too, into a beaver!"
Cautiously replied the beaver,
70   With reserve he thus made answer:
"Let me first consult the others,

Let me ask the other beavers."
Down he sank into the water,
Heavily sank he, as a stone sinks,
75   Down among the leaves and branches,
Brown and matted at the bottom.
      On the dam stood Pau-Puk-Keewis,
O'er his ankles flowed the streamlet,
Spouted through the chinks below him,
80   Dashed upon the stones beneath him,
Spread serene and calm before him,
And the sunshine and the shadows
Fell in flecks and gleams upon him,
Fell in little shining patches,
85   Through the waving, rustling branches.
      From the bottom rose the beavers,
Silently above the surface
Rose one head and then another,
Till the pond seemed full of beavers,
90   Full of black and shining faces.
      To the beavers Pau-Puk-Keewis
Spake entreating, said in this wise:
"Very pleasant is your dwelling,
O my friends! and safe from danger;
95   Can you not with all your cunning,
All your wisdom and contrivance,
Change me, too, into a beaver?"
      "Yes!" replied Ahmeek, the beaver,
He the King of all the beavers,
100   "Let yourself slide down among us,
Down into the tranquil water."
      Down into the pond among them
Silently sank Pau-Puk-Keewis;
Black became his shirt of deer-skin,
105   Black his moccasins and leggins,
In a broad black tail behind him
Spread his fox-tails and his fringes;
He was changed into a beaver.
      "Make me large," said Pau-Puk-Keewis,
110   "Make me large and make me larger,
Larger than the other beavers."
"Yes," the beaver chief responded,

"When our lodge below you enter,
In our wigwam we will make you
115   Ten times larger than the others."
       Thus into the clear brown water
Silently sank Pau-Puk-Keewis;
Found the bottom covered over
With the trunks of trees and branches,
120   Hoards of food against the winter,
Piles and heaps against the famine,
Found the lodge with arching doorway,
Leading into spacious chambers.
       Here they made him large and larger,
125   Made him largest of the beavers,
Ten times larger than the others.
"You shall be our ruler," said they;
"Chief and king of all the beavers."
       But not long had Pau-Puk-Keewis
130   Sat in state among the beavers,
When there came a voice of warning
From the watchman at his station
In the water-flags and lilies,
Saying, "Here is Hiawatha!
135   Hiawatha with his hunters!"
       Then they heard a cry above them,
Heard a shouting and a tramping,
Heard a crashing and a rushing,
And the water round and o'er them
140   Sank and sucked away in eddies,
And they knew their dam was broken.
       On the lodge's roof the hunters
Leaped, and broke it all asunder;
Streamed the sunshine through the crevice,
145   Sprang the beavers through the doorway,
Hid themselves in deeper water,
In the channel of the streamlet;
But the mighty Pau-Puk-Keewis
Could not pass beneath the doorway;
150   He was puffed with pride and feeding,
He was swollen like a bladder.
       Through the roof looked Hiawatha,
Cried aloud, "O Pau-Puk-Keewis!

Vain are all your craft and cunning,
155 Vain your manifold disguises!
Well I know you, Pau-Puk-Keewis!"
With their clubs they beat and bruised him,
Beat to death poor Pau-Puk-Keewis,
Pounded him as maize is pounded,
160 Till his skull was crushed to pieces.
   Six tall hunters, lithe and limber,
Bore him home on poles and branches,
Bore the body of the beaver;
But the ghost, the Jeebi in him,
165 Thought and felt as Pau-Puk-Keewis,
Still lived on as Pau-Puk-Keewis.
   And it fluttered, strove, and struggled,
Waving hither, waving thither,
As the curtains of a wigwam
170 Struggle with their thongs of deer-skin,
When the wintry wind is blowing;
Till it drew itself together,
Till it rose up from the body,
Till it took the form and features
175 Of the cunning Pau-Puk-Keewis
Vanishing into the forest.
   But the wary Hiawatha
Saw the figure ere it vanished,
Saw the form of Pau-Puk-Keewis
180 Glide into the soft blue shadow
Of the pine-trees of the forest;
Toward the squares of white beyond it,
Toward an opening in the forest,
Like a wind it rushed and panted,
185 Bending all the boughs before it,
And behind it, as the rain comes,
Came the steps of Hiawatha.
   To a lake with many islands
Came the breathless Pau-Puk-Keewis,
190 Where among the water-lilies
Pishnekuh, the brant, were sailing;
Through the tufts of rushes floating,
Steering through the reedy islands.
Now their broad black beaks they lifted,

195   Now they plunged beneath the water,
Now they darkened in the shadow,
Now they brightened in the sunshine.
      "Pishnekuh!" cried Pau-Puk-Keewis,
"Pishnekuh! my brothers!" said he,
200   "Change me to a brant with plumage,
With a shining neck and feathers,
Make me large, and make me larger,
Ten times larger than the others."
      Straightway to a brant they changed him,
205   With two huge and dusky pinions,
With a bosom smooth and rounded,
With a bill like two great paddles,
Made him larger than the others,
Ten times larger than the largest,
210   Just as, shouting from the forest,
On the shore stood Hiawatha.
      Up they rose with cry and clamor,
With a whirr and beat of pinions,
Rose up from the reedy islands,
215   From the water-flags and lilies.
And they said to Pau-Puk-Keewis:
"In your flying, look not downward,
Take good heed, and look not downward,
Lest some strange mischance should happen,
220   Lest some great mishap befall you!"
      Fast and far they fled to northward,
Fast and far through mist and sunshine,
Fed among the moors and fen-lands,
Slept among the reeds and rushes.
225   On the morrow as they journeyed,
Buoyed and lifted by the South-wind,
Wafted onward by the South-wind,
Blowing fresh and strong behind them,
Rose a sound of human voices
230   Rose a clamor from beneath them,
From the lodges of a village,
From the people miles beneath them.
      For the people of the village
Saw the flock of brant with wonder,
235   Saw the wings of Pau-Puk-Keewis

Flapping far up in the ether,
Broader than two doorway curtains.
     Pau-Puk-Keewis heard the shouting,
Knew the voice of Hiawatha,
240   Knew the outcry of Iagoo,
And, forgetful of the warning,
Drew his neck in, and looked downward,
And the wind that blew behind him
Caught his mighty fan of feathers,
245   Sent him wheeling, whirling downward!
     All in vain did Pau-Puk-Keewis
Struggle to regain his balance!
Whirling round and round and downward,
He beheld in turn the village
250   And in turn the flock above him,
Saw the village coming nearer,
And the flock receding farther,
Heard the voices growing louder,
Heard the shouting and the laughter;
255   Saw no more the flock above him,
Only saw the earth beneath him;
Dead out of the empty heaven,
Dead among the shouting people,
With a heavy sound and sullen,
260   Fell the brant with broken pinions.
     But his soul, his ghost, his shadow,
Still survived as Pau-Puk-Keewis,
Took again the form and features
Of the handsome Yenadizze,
265   And again went rushing onward,
Followed fast by Hiawatha,
Crying: "Not so wide the world is,
Not so long and rough the way is,
But my wrath shall overtake you,
270   But my vengeance shall attain you!"
     And so near he came, so near him,
That his hand was stretched to seize him,
His right hand to seize and hold him,
When the cunning Pau-Puk-Keewis
275   Whirled and spun about in circles,
Fanned the air into a whirlwind,

Danced the dust and leaves about him,
And amid the whirling eddies
Sprang into a hollow oak-tree,
280   Changed himself into a serpent,
Gliding out through root and rubbish.
      With his right hand Hiawatha
Smote amain the hollow oak-tree,
Rent it into shreds and splinters,
285   Left it lying there in fragments.
But in vain; for Pau-Puk-Keewis,
Once again in human figure,
Full in sight ran on before him,
Sped away in gust and whirlwind,
290   On the shores of Gitche Gumee,
Westward by the Big-Sea-Water,
Came unto the rocky headlands,
To the Pictured Rocks of sandstone,
Looking over lake and landscape.
295   And the Old Man of the Mountain,
He the Manito of Mountains,
Opened wide his rocky doorways,
Opened wide his deep abysses,
Giving Pau-Puk-Keewis shelter
300   In his caverns dark and dreary,
Bidding Pau-Puk-Keewis welcome
To his gloomy lodge of sandstone.
      There without stood Hiawatha,
Found the doorways closed against him,
305   With his mittens, Minjekahwun,
Smote great caverns in the sandstone,
Cried aloud in tones of thunder,
"Open! I am Hiawatha!"
But the Old Man of the Mountain
310   Opened not, and made no answer
From the silent crags of sandstone,
From the gloomy rock abysses.
      Then he raised his hands to heaven,
Called imploring on the tempest,
315   Called Waywassimo, the lightning,
And the thunder, Annemeekee;
And they came with night and darkness,

Sweeping down the Big-Sea-Water
From the distant Thunder Mountains;
320   And the trembling Pau-Puk-Keewis
Heard the footsteps of the thunder,
Saw the red eyes of the lightning,
Was afraid, and crouched and trembled.
      Then Waywassimo, the lightning,
325   Smote the doorways of the caverns,
With his war-club smote the doorways,
Smote the jutting crags of sandstone,
And the thunder, Annemeekee,
Shouted down into the caverns,
330   Saying, "Where is Pau-Puk-Keewis!"
And the crags fell, and beneath them
Dead among the rocky ruins
Lay the cunning Pau-Puk-Keewis,
Lay the handsome Yenadizze,
335   Slain in his own human figure.
      Ended were his wild adventures,
Ended were his tricks and gambols,
Ended all his craft and cunning,
Ended all his mischief-making,
340   All his gambling and his dancing,
All his wooing of the maidens.
      Then the noble Hiawatha
Took his soul, his ghost, his shadow,
Spake and said: "O Pau-Puk-Keewis,
345   Never more in human figure
Shall you search for new adventures;
Never more with jest and laughter
Dance the dust and leaves in whirlwinds;
But above there in the heavens
350   You shall soar and sail in circles;
I will change you to an eagle,
To Keneu, the great war-eagle,
Chief of all the fowls with feathers,
Chief of Hiawatha's chickens."
355   And the name of Pau-Puk-Keewis
Lingers still among the people,
Lingers still among the singers,
And among the story-tellers;

And in Winter, when the snow-flakes
360   Whirl in eddies round the lodges,
When the wind in gusty tumult
O'er the smoke-flue pipes and whistles,
"There," they cry, "comes Pau-Puk-Keewis;
He is dancing through the village,
365   He is gathering in his harvest!"

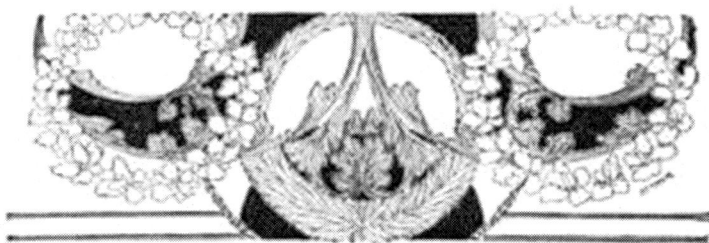

XVIII. - THE DEATH OF KWASIND.

Far and wide among the nations
Spread the name and fame of Kwasind;
No man dared to strive with Kwasind,
No man could compete with Kwasind.
5 But the mischievous Puk-Wudjies,
They the envious Little People,
They the fairies and the pygmies,
Plotted and conspired against him.
"If this hateful Kwasind," said they,
10 "If this great, outrageous fellow
Goes on thus a little longer,
Tearing everything he touches,
Rending everything to pieces,
Filling all the world with wonder,
15 What becomes of the Puk-Wudjies?
Who will care for the Puk-Wudjies?
He will tread us down like mushrooms,
Drive us all into the water,
Give our bodies to be eaten
20 By the wicked Nee-ba-naw-baigs,
By the Spirits of the water!"
So the angry Little People
All conspired against the Strong Man,
All conspired to murder Kwasind,
25 Yes, to rid the world of Kwasind,
The audacious, overbearing,
Heartless, haughty, dangerous Kwasind!
Now this wondrous strength of Kwasind
In his crown alone was seated;

30   In his crown too was his weakness:
There alone could he be wounded,
Nowhere else could weapon pierce him,
Nowhere else could weapon harm him.
     Even there the only weapon
35   That could wound him, that could slay him,
Was the seed-cone of the pine-tree,
Was the blue cone of the fir-tree.
This was Kwasind's fatal secret,
Known to no man among mortals;
40   But the cunning Little People,
The Puk-Wudjies, knew the secret,
Knew the only way to kill him.
     So they gathered cones together,
Gathered seed-cones of the pine-tree,
45   Gathered blue cones of the fir-tree,
In the woods by Taquamenaw,
Brought them to the river's margin,
Heaped them in great piles together,
Where the red rocks from the margin
50   Jutting overhang the river.
There they lay in wait for Kwasind,
The malicious Little People.
     'T was an afternoon in Summer;
Very hot and still the air was,
55   Very smooth the gliding river,
Motionless the sleeping shadows:
Insects glistened in the sunshine,
Insects skated on the water
Filled the drowsy air with buzzing,
60   With a far-resounding war-cry.
     Down the river came the Strong Man,
In his birch canoe came Kwasind,
Floating slowly down the current
Of the sluggish Taquamenaw,
65   Very languid with the weather,
Very sleepy with the silence.
     From the overhanging branches,
From the tassels of the birch-trees,
Soft the Spirit of Sleep descended;
70   By his airy hosts surrounded,

His invisible attendants,
Came the Spirit of Sleep, Nepahwin;
Like the burnished Dush-kwo-ne-she,
Like a dragon fly, he hovered
75　O'er the drowsy head of Kwasind.
　　　　To his ear there came a murmur
As of waves upon a sea-shore,
As of far-off tumbling waters,
As of winds among the pine-trees;
80　And he felt upon his forehead
Blows of little airy war-clubs,
Wielded by the slumbrous legions
Of the Spirit of Sleep, Nepahwin,
As of some one breathing on him.
85　　　　At the first blow of their war-clubs,
Fell a drowsiness on Kwasind;
At the second blow they smote him,
Motionless his paddle rested;
At the third, before his vision
90　Reeled the landscape into darkness,
Very sound asleep was Kwasind.
　　　　So he floated down the river,
Like a blind man seated upright,
Floated down the Taquamenaw,
95　Underneath the trembling birch-trees,
Underneath the wooded headlands,
Underneath the war encampment
Of the pygmies, the Puk-Wudjies.
　　　　There they stood, all armed and waiting,
100　Hurled the pine-cones down upon him,
Struck him on his brawny shoulders,
On his crown defenseless struck him.
"Death to Kwasind!" was the sudden
War-cry of the Little People.
105　　　　And he sideways swayed and tumbled,
Sideways fell into the river,
Plunged beneath the sluggish water
Headlong, as an otter plunges;
And the birch canoe, abandoned,
110　Drifted empty down the river,
Bottom upward swerved and drifted:

Nothing more was seen of Kwasind.

"There they stood, all armed and waiting,
Hurled the pine-cones down upon him."

But the memory of the Strong Man
Lingered long among the people,
115   And whenever through the forest
Raged and roared the wintry tempest,
And the branches, tossed and troubled,
Creaked and groaned and split asunder,
"Kwasind!" cried they; "that is Kwasind!
120   He is gathering in his fire-wood!"

Strings of Black and White Wampum Shells.

XIX. - THE GHOSTS.

Never stoops the soaring vulture
On his quarry in the desert,
On the sick or wounded bison,
But another vulture, watching
5 From his high aerial look-out,
Sees the downward plunge, and follows;
And a third pursues the second,
Coming from the invisible ether,
First a speck, and then a vulture,
10 Till the air is dark with pinions.
  So disasters come not singly;
But as if they watched and waited,
Scanning one another's motions,
When the first descends, the others
15 Follow, follow, gathering flock-wise
Round their victim, sick and wounded,
First a shadow, then a sorrow,
Till the air is dark with anguish.
  Now, o'er all the dreary Northland,
20 Mighty Peboan, the Winter,
Breathing on the lakes and rivers,
Into stone had changed their waters.
From his hair he shook the snow-flakes,
Till the plains were strewn with whiteness,
25 One uninterrupted level,
As if, stooping, the Creator
With his hand had smoothed them over.
  Through the forest, wide and wailing,
Roamed the hunter on his snow-shoes;

30	In the village worked the women,
	Pounded maize, or dressed the deer-skin;
	And the young men played together
	On the ice the noisy ball-play,
	On the plain the dance of snow-shoes.
35	One dark evening, after sundown,
	In her wigwam Laughing Water
	Sat with old Nokomis, waiting
	For the steps of Hiawatha
	Homeward from the hunt returning.
40	On their faces gleamed the fire-light,
	Painting them with streaks of crimson,
	In the eyes of old Nokomis
	Glimmered like the watery moonlight,
	In the eyes of Laughing Water
45	Glistened like the sun in water;
	And behind them crouched their shadows
	In the corners of the wigwam,
	And the smoke in wreaths above them
	Climbed and crowded through the smoke-flue.
50	Then the curtain of the doorway
	From without was slowly lifted;
	Brighter glowed the fire a moment,
	And a moment swerved the smoke-wreath,
	As two women entered softly,
55	Passed the doorway uninvited,
	Without word of salutation,
	Without sign of recognition,
	Sat down in the farthest corner,
	Crouching low among the shadows.
60	From their aspect and their garments,
	Strangers seemed they in the village;
	Very pale and haggard were they,
	As they sat there sad and silent,
	Trembling, cowering with the shadows.
65	Was it the wind above the smoke-flue,
	Muttering down into the wigwam?
	Was it the owl, the Koko-koho,
	Hooting from the dismal forest?
	Sure a voice said in the silence:
70	"These are corpses clad in garments,

These are ghosts that come to haunt you,
From the kingdom of Ponemah,
From the land of the Hereafter!"
  Homeward now came Hiawatha
75 From his hunting in the forest,
With the snow upon his tresses,
And the red deer on his shoulders.
At the feet of Laughing Water
Down he threw his lifeless burden;
80 Nobler, handsomer she thought him,
Than when first he came to woo her,
First threw down the deer before her,
As a token of his wishes,
As a promise of the future.
85 Then he turned and saw the strangers,
Cowering, crouching with the shadows;
Said within himself, "Who are they?
What strange guests has Minnehaha?"
But he questioned not the strangers,
90 Only spake to bid them welcome
To his lodge, his food, his fireside.
  When the evening meal was ready,
And the deer had been divided,
Both the pallid guests, the strangers,
95 Springing from among the shadows,
Seized upon the choicest portions,
Seized the white fat of the roebuck,
Set apart for Laughing Water,
For the wife of Hiawatha;
100 Without asking, without thanking,
Eagerly devoured the morsels,
Flitted back among the shadows
In the corner of the wigwam.
  Not a word spake Hiawatha,
105 Not a motion made Nokomis,
Not a gesture Laughing Water;
Not a change came o'er their features;
Only Minnehaha softly
Whispered, saying, "They are famished;
110 Let them do what best delights them;
Let them eat, for they are famished."

Many a daylight dawned and darkened,
Many a night shook off the daylight
As the pine shakes off the snow-flakes
115 From the midnight of its branches;
Day by day the guests unmoving
Sat there silent in the wigwam;
But by night, in storm or starlight,
Forth they went into the forest,
120 Bringing fire-wood to the wigwam,
Bringing pine-cones for the burning,
Always sad and always silent.
And whenever Hiawatha
Came from fishing or from hunting,
125 When the evening meal was ready,
And the food had been divided,
Gliding from their darksome corner,
Came the pallid guests, the strangers,
Seized upon the choicest portions
130 Set aside for Laughing Water,
And without rebuke or question
Flitted back among the shadows.
Never once had Hiawatha
By a word or look reproved them;
135 Never once had old Nokomis
Made a gesture of impatience;
Never once had Laughing Water
Shown resentment at the outrage.
All had they endured in silence,
140 That the rights of guest and stranger,
That the virtue of free-giving,
By a look might not be lessened,
By a word might not be broken.
Once at midnight Hiawatha,
145 Ever wakeful, ever watchful,
In the wigwam, dimly lighted
By the brands that still were burning,
By the glimmering, flickering fire-light,
Heard a sighing, oft repeated,
150 Heard a sobbing as of sorrow.
From his couch rose Hiawatha,
From his shaggy hides of bison,

Pushed aside the deer-skin curtain,
Saw the pallid guests, the shadows,
155   Sitting upright on their couches,
Weeping in the silent midnight.
        And he said: "O guests! why is it
That your hearts are so afflicted,
That you sob so in the midnight?
160   Has perchance the old Nokomis,
Has my wife, my Minnehaha,
Wronged or grieved you by unkindness,
Failed in hospitable duties?"

Indian Burial

        Then the shadows ceased from weeping,
165   Ceased from sobbing and lamenting,
And they said, with gentle voices:
"We are ghosts of the departed,
Souls of those who once were with you.
From the realms of Chibiabos
170   Hither have we come to try you,

Hither have we come to warn you.
     "Cries of grief and lamentation
Reach us in the Blessed Islands:
Cries of anguish from the living,
175   Calling back their friends departed,
Sadden us with useless sorrow.
Therefore have we come to try you;
No one knows us, no one heeds us.
We are but a burden to you,
180   And we see that the departed
Have no place among the living.
     "Think of this, O Hiawatha!
Speak of it to all the people,
That henceforward and forever
185   They no more with lamentations
Sadden the souls of the departed
In the Islands of the Blessed.
     "Do not lay such heavy burdens
In the graves of those you bury,
190   Not such weight of furs and wampum,
Not such weight of pots and kettles,
For the spirits faint beneath them.
Only give them food to carry,
Only give them fire to light them.
195   "Four days is the spirit's journey
To the land of ghosts and shadows,
Four its lonely night encampments;
Four times must their fires be lighted.
Therefore, when the dead are buried,
200   Let a fire, as night approaches,
Four times on the grave be kindled,
That the soul upon its journey
May not lack the cheerful fire-light,
May not grope about in darkness.
205   "Farewell, noble Hiawatha!
We have put you to the trial,
To the proof have put your patience,
By the insult of our presence,
By the outrage of our actions.
210   We have found you great and noble.
Fail not in the greater trial,

Faint not in the harder struggle."
  When they ceased, a sudden darkness
Fell and filled the silent wigwam.
215 Hiawatha heard a rustle
As of garments trailing by him,
Heard the curtain of the doorway
Lifted by a hand he saw not,
Felt the cold breath of the night air,
220 For a moment saw the starlight;
But he saw the ghosts no longer,
Saw no more the wandering spirits
From the kingdom of Ponemah,
From the land of the Hereafter.

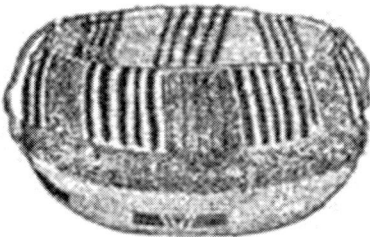

Indian Baskets, Decorated with Feathers and Quills.

XX. - THE FAMINE.

O the long and dreary Winter!
O the cold and cruel Winter!
Ever thicker, thicker, thicker
Froze the ice on lake and river,
Ever deeper, deeper, deeper,
Fell the snow o'er all the landscape,
Fell the covering snow, and drifted
Through the forest, round the village.
        Hardly from his buried wigwam
Could the hunter force a passage;
With his mittens and his snow-shoes
Vainly walked he through the forest,
Sought for bird or beast and found none,
Saw no track of deer or rabbit,
In the snow beheld no footprints,
In the ghastly, gleaming forest
Fell, and could not rise from weakness,
Perished there from cold and hunger.
        O the famine and the fever!
O the wasting of the famine!
O the blasting of the fever!
O the wailing of the children!
O the anguish of the women!
        All the earth was sick and famished;
Hungry was the air around them,
Hungry was the sky above them,
And the hungry stars in heaven
Like the eyes of wolves glared at them!
        Into Hiawatha's wigwam

30   Came two other guests as silent
      As the ghosts were, and as gloomy,
      Waited not to be invited,
      Did not parley at the doorway,
      Sat there without word of welcome
35   In the seat of Laughing Water;
      Looked with haggard eyes and hollow
      At the face of Laughing Water.
           And the foremost said: "Behold me!
      I am Famine, Bukadawin!"
40   And the other said: "Behold me!
      I am Fever, Ahkosewin!"
           And the lovely Minnehaha
      Shuddered as they looked upon her,
      Shuddered at the words they uttered,
45   Lay down on her bed in silence,
      Hid her face, but made no answer;
      Lay there trembling, freezing, burning
      At the looks they cast upon her,
      At the fearful words they uttered.
50   Forth into the empty forest
      Rushed the maddened Hiawatha;
      In his heart was deadly sorrow,
      In his face a stony firmness;
      On his brow the sweat of anguish
55   Started, but it froze and fell not.
           Wrapped in furs and armed for hunting,
      With his mighty bow of ash-tree,
      With his quiver full of arrows,
      With his mittens, Minjekahwun,
60   Into the vast and vacant forest
      On his snow-shoes strode he forward.
           "Gitche Manito, the Mighty!"
      Cried he with his face uplifted
      In that bitter hour of anguish,
65   "Give your children food, O father!
      Give us food, or we must perish!
      Give me food for Minnehaha,
      For my dying Minnehaha!"
           Through the far-resounding forest,
70   Through the forest vast and vacant

Rang that cry of desolation,
But there came no other answer
Than the echo of his crying,
Than the echo of the woodlands,
75   "Minnehaha! Minnehaha!"
        All day long roved Hiawatha
In that melancholy forest,
Through the shadow of whose thickets,
In the pleasant days of Summer,
80   Of that ne'er forgotten Summer,
He had brought his young wife homeward
From the land of the Dacotahs;
When the birds sang in the thickets,
And the streamlets laughed and glistened,
85   And the air was full of fragrance,
And the lovely Laughing Water
Said with voice that did not tremble,
"I will follow you, my husband!"
        In the wigwam with Nokomis,
90   With those gloomy guests that watched her,
With the Famine and the Fever,
She was lying, the Beloved,
She the dying Minnehaha.
        "Hark!" she said; "I hear a rushing,
95   Hear a roaring and a rushing,
Hear the Falls of Minnehaha
Calling to me from a distance!"
"No, my child!" said old Nokomis,
"'T is the night-wind in the pine-trees!"
100   "Look!" she said; "I see my father
Standing lonely at his doorway,
Beckoning to me from his wigwam
In the land of the Dacotahs!"
"No, my child!" said old Nokomis,
105   "'T is the smoke, that waves and beckons!"
        "Ah!" said she, "the eyes of Pauguk
Glare upon me in the darkness,
I can feel his icy fingers
Clasping mine amid the darkness!
110   Hiawatha! Hiawatha!"
        And the desolate Hiawatha,

Far away amid the forest,
Miles away among the mountains,
Heard that sudden cry of anguish,
115   Heard the voice of Minnehaha
Calling to him in the darkness,
"Hiawatha! Hiawatha!"
     Over snow-fields waste and pathless,
Under snow-encumbered branches,
120   Homeward hurried Hiawatha,
Empty-handed, heavy-hearted,
Heard Nokomis moaning, wailing:
"Wahonowin! Wahonowin!
Would that I had perished for you,
125   Would that I were dead as you are!
Wahonowin! Wahonowin!"
     And he rushed into the wigwam,
Saw the old Nokomis slowly
Rocking to and fro and moaning,
130   Saw his lovely Minnehaha
Lying dead and cold before him,
And his bursting heart within him
Uttered such a cry of anguish,
That the forest moaned and shuddered,
135   That the very stars in heaven
Shook and trembled with his anguish.
     Then he sat down, still and speechless,
On the bed of Minnehaha,
At the feet of Laughing Water,
140   At those willing feet, that never
More would lightly run to meet him,
Never more would lightly follow.
     With both hands his face he covered,
Seven long days and nights he sat there,
145   As if in a swoon he sat there,
Speechless, motionless, unconscious
Of the daylight or the darkness.
     Then they buried Minnehaha;
In the snow a grave they made her,
150   In the forest deep and darksome,
Underneath the moaning hemlocks;
Clothed her in her richest garments,

Wrapped her in her robes of ermine,
Covered her with snow, like ermine;
155   Thus they buried Minnehaha.
        And at night a fire was lighted,
On her grave four times was kindled,
For her soul upon its journey
To the Islands of the Blessed.
160   From his doorway Hiawatha
Saw it burning in the forest,
Lighting up the gloomy hemlocks;
From his sleepless bed uprising,
From the bed of Minnehaha,
165   Stood and watched it at the doorway,
That it might not be extinguished,
Might not leave her in the darkness.
        "Farewell!" said he, "Minnehaha!
Farewell, O my Laughing Water!
170   All my heart is buried with you,
All my thoughts go onward with you!
Come not back again to labor,
Come not back again to suffer,
Where the Famine and the Fever
175   Wear the heart and waste the body.
Soon my task will be completed,
Soon your footsteps I shall follow
To the Islands of the Blessed,
To the Kingdom of Ponemah,
180   To the Land of the Hereafter!"

XXI. - THE WHITE MAN'S FOOT.

In his lodge beside a river,
Close beside a frozen river,
Sat an old man, sad and lonely.
White his hair was as a snow-drift;
5   Dull and low his fire was burning,
And the old man shook and trembled,
Folded in his Waubewyon,
In his tattered white-skin-wrapper,
Hearing nothing but the tempest
10   As it roared along the forest,
Seeing nothing but the snow-storm,
As it whirled and hissed and drifted.
     All the coals were white with ashes,
And the fire was slowly dying,
15   As a young man, walking lightly,
At the open doorway entered.
Red with blood of youth his cheeks were,
Soft his eyes, as stars in Spring-time,
Bound his forehead was with grasses,
20   Bound and plumed with scented grasses;
On his lips a smile of beauty,
Filling all the lodge with sunshine,
In his hand a bunch of blossoms
Filling all the lodge with sweetness.
25   "Ah, my son!" exclaimed the old man,
"Happy are my eyes to see you.
Sit here on the mat beside me,
Sit here by the dying embers,
Let us pass the night together.

30   Tell me of your strange adventures,
      Of the lands where you have travelled;
      I will tell you of my prowess,
      Of my many deeds of wonder."
            From his pouch he drew his peace-pipe,
35   Very old and strangely fashioned;
      Made of red stone was the pipe-head,
      And the stem a reed with feathers;
      Filled the pipe with bark of willow,
      Placed a burning coal upon it,
40   Gave it to his guest, the stranger,
      And began to speak in this wise:
      "When I blow my breath about me,
      When I breathe upon the landscape,
      Motionless are all the rivers,
45   Hard as stone becomes the water!"
            And the young man answered, smiling:
      "When I blow my breath about me,
      When I breathe upon the landscape,
      Flowers spring up o'er all the meadows,
50   Singing, onward rush the rivers!"
            "When I shake my hoary tresses,"
      Said the old man, darkly frowning,
      "All the land with snow is covered;
      All the leaves from all the branches
55   Fall and fade and die and wither,
      For I breathe, and lo! they are not.
      From the waters and the marshes
      Rise the wild goose and the heron,
      Fly away to distant regions,
60   For I speak, and lo! they are not.
      And where'er my footsteps wander,
      All the wild beasts of the forest
      Hide themselves in holes and caverns,
      And the earth becomes as flintstone!"
65   "When I shake my flowing ringlets,"
      Said the young man, softly laughing,
      "Showers of rain fall warm and welcome,
      Plants lift up their heads rejoicing,
      Back unto their lakes and marshes
70   Come the wild goose and the heron,

Homeward shoots the arrowy swallow,
Sing the bluebird and the robin,
And where'er my footsteps wander,
All the meadows wave with blossoms,
75   All the woodlands ring with music,
All the trees are dark with foliage!"
       While they spake, the night departed:
From the distant realms of Wabun,
From his shining lodge of silver,
80   Like a warrior robed and painted,
Came the sun, and said, "Behold me!
Gheezis, the great sun, behold me!"
       Then the old man's tongue was speechless
And the air grew warm and pleasant,
85   And upon the wigwam sweetly
Sang the bluebird and the robin,
And the stream began to murmur,
And a scent of growing grasses
Through the lodge was gently wafted.
90   And Segwun, the youthful stranger,
More distinctly in the daylight
Saw the icy face before him;
It was Peboan, the Winter!
       From his eyes the tears were flowing,
95   As from melting lakes the streamlets,
And his body shrunk and dwindled
As the shouting sun ascended,
Till into the air it faded,
Till into the ground it vanished,
100   And the young man saw before him,
On the hearth-stone of the wigwam,
Where the fire had smoked and smouldered,
Saw the earliest flower of Spring-time,
Saw the Beauty of the Spring-time,
105   Saw the Miskodeed in blossom.
       Thus it was that in the North-land
After that unheard-of coldness,
That intolerable Winter,
Came the Spring with all its splendor,
110   All its birds and all its blossoms,
All its flowers and leaves and grasses.

Sailing on the wind to northward,
Flying in great flocks, like arrows,
Like huge arrows shot through heaven,
115 Passed the swan, the Mahnahbezee,
Speaking almost as a man speaks;
And in long lines waving, bending
Like a bow-string snapped asunder,
Came the white goose, Waw-be-wawa;
120 And in pairs, or singly flying,
Mahng the loon, with clangorous pinions,
The blue heron, the Shuh-shuh-gah,
And the grouse, the Mushkodasa.
In the thickets and the meadows
125 Piped the bluebird, the Owaissa,
On the summit of the lodges
Sang the Opechee, the robin,
In the covert of the pine-trees
Cooed the pigeon, the Omemee,
130 And the sorrowing Hiawatha,
Speechless in his infinite sorrow,
Heard their voices calling to him,
Went forth from his gloomy doorway,
Stood and gazed into the heaven,
135 Gazed upon the earth and waters.
From his wanderings far to eastward,
From the regions of the morning,
From the shining land of Wabun,
Homeward now returned Iagoo,
140 The great traveller, the great boaster,
Full of new and strange adventures,
Marvels many and many wonders.
And the people of the village
Listened to him as he told them
145 Of his marvellous adventures,
Laughing answered him in this wise:
"Ugh! it is indeed Iagoo!
No one else beholds such wonders!"
He had seen, he said, a water
150 Bigger than the Big-Sea-Water,
Broader than the Gitche Gumee,
Bitter so that none could drink it!

At each other looked the warriors,
Looked the women at each other,
155 Smiled, and said, "It cannot be so!
Kaw!" they said, "it cannot be so!"
    O'er it, said he, o'er this water

Came a great canoe with pinions,
A canoe with wings came flying,
160 Bigger than a grove of pine-trees,
Taller than the tallest tree-tops!
And the old men and the women
Looked and tittered at each other;
"Kaw!" they said, "we don't believe it!"
165   From its mouth, he said, to greet him,
Came Waywassimo, the lightning,
Came the thunder, Annemeekee!
And the warriors and the women
Laughed aloud at poor Iagoo;
170 "Kaw!" they said, "what tales you tell us!"
    In it, said he, came a people,
In the great canoe with pinions
Came, he said, a hundred warriors;
Painted white were all their faces,
175 And with hair their chins were covered!
And the warriors and the women
Laughed and shouted in derision,

Like the ravens on the tree-tops,
Like the crows upon the hemlocks.
180 "Kaw!" they said, "what lies you tell us!
Do not think that we believe them!"
Only Hiawatha laughed not,
But he gravely spake and answered
To their jeering and their jesting:
185 "True is all Iagoo tells us;
I have seen it in a vision,
Seen the great canoe with pinions,
Seen the people with white faces,
Seen the coming of this bearded
190 People of the wooden vessel
From the regions of the morning,
From the shining land of Wabun.
"Gitche Manito the Mighty,
The Great Spirit, the Creator,
195 Sends them hither on his errand,
Sends them to us with his message.
Wheresoe'er they move, before them
Swarms the stinging fly, the Ahmo,
Swarms the bee, the honey-maker;
200 Wheresoe'er they tread, beneath them
Springs a flower unknown among us,
Springs the White-man's Foot in blossom.
"Let us welcome, then, the strangers,
Hail them as our friends and brothers,
205 And the heart's right hand of friendship
Give them when they come to see us.
Gitche Manito, the Mighty,
Said this to me in my vision.
"I beheld, too, in that vision
210 All the secrets of the future,
Of the distant days that shall be.
I beheld the westward marches
Of the unknown, crowded nations.
All the land was full of people,

215 Restless, struggling, toiling, striving,
  Speaking many tongues, yet feeling
  But one heart-beat in their bosoms.
  In the woodlands rang their axes,
  Smoked their towns in all the valleys,
220 Over all the lakes and rivers
  Rushed their great canoes of thunder.
   "Then a darker, drearier vision
  Passed before me, vague and cloud-like:
  I beheld our nation scattered,
225 All forgetful of my counsels,
  Weakened, warring with each other;
  Saw the remnants of our people
  Sweeping westward, wild and woful,
  Like the cloud-rack of a tempest,
230 Like the withered leaves of Autumn!"

XXII. - HIAWATHA'S DEPARTURE.

By the shore of Gitche Gumee,
By the shining Big-Sea-Water,
At the doorway of his wigwam,
In the pleasant summer morning,
Hiawatha stood and waited.
All the air was full of freshness,
All the earth was bright and joyous,
And before him, through the sunshine,
Westward toward the neighboring forest
10 Passed in golden swarms the Ahmo,
Passed the bees, the honey-makers,
Burning, singing in the sunshine.
    Bright above him shone the heavens,
Level spread the lake before him;
15 From its bosom leaped the sturgeon,
Sparkling, flashing in the sunshine;
On its margin the great forest
Stood reflected in the water,
Every tree-top had its shadow,
20 Motionless beneath the water.
        From the brow of Hiawatha
Gone was every trace of sorrow,
As the fog from off the water,
As the mist from off the meadow.
25 With a smile of joy and triumph,
With a look of exultation,
As of one who in a vision
Sees what is to be, but is not,
Stood and waited Hiawatha.

30   Toward the sun his hands were lifted,
Both the palms spread out against it,
And between the parted fingers
Fell the sunshine on his features,
Flecked with light his naked shoulders,
35   As it falls and flecks an oak-tree
Through the rifted leaves and branches.
          O'er the water floating, flying,
Something in the hazy distance,
Something in the mists of morning,
40   Loomed and lifted from the water,
Now seemed floating, now seemed flying,
Coming nearer, nearer, nearer.
          Was it Shingebis the diver?
Was it the pelican, the Shada?
45   Or the heron, the Shuh-shuh-gah?
Or the white goose, Waw-be-wawa,
With the water dripping, flashing
From its glossy neck and feathers?
          It was neither goose nor diver,
50   Neither pelican nor heron,
O'er the water, floating, flying,
Through the shining mist of morning,
But a birch canoe with paddles,
Rising, sinking on the water,
55   Dripping, flashing in the sunshine;
And within it came a people
From the distant land of Wabun,
From the farthest realms of morning
Came the Black-Robe chief, the Prophet,
60   He the Priest of Prayer, the Pale-face,
With his guides and his companions.
          And the noble Hiawatha,
With his hands aloft extended,
Held aloft in sign of welcome,
65   Waited, full of exultation,
Till the birch canoe with paddles
Grated on the shining pebbles,
Stranded on the sandy margin,
Till the Black-Robe chief, the Pale-face,
70   With the cross upon his bosom,

Landed on the sandy margin.
Then the joyous Hiawatha
Cried aloud and spake in this wise:
"Beautiful is the sun, O strangers,
75   When you come so far to see us!
All our town in peace awaits you;
All our doors stand open for you;

You shall enter all our wigwams,
For the heart's right hand we give you.
80   "Never bloomed the earth so gayly,
Never shone the sun so brightly,
As to-day they shine and blossom
When you come so far to see us!
Never was our lake so tranquil,
85   Nor so free from rocks and sand-bars;
For your birch canoe in passing
Has removed both rock and sand-bar.
"Never before had our tobacco
Such a sweet and pleasant flavor,
90   Never the broad leaves of our corn-fields
Were so beautiful to look on,
As they seem to us this morning,
When you come so far to see us!"
And the Black-Robe chief made answer,
95   Stammered in his speech a little,

Speaking words yet unfamiliar:
"Peace be with you, Hiawatha,
Peace be with you and your people,
Peace of prayer, and peace of pardon,
100   Peace of Christ, and joy of Mary!"

NAVAJO MATRON WEAVING A BLANKET.
"Bring a wife with nimble fingers,
Heart and hand that move together."

Then the generous Hiawatha
Led the strangers to his wigwam,
Seated them on skins of bison,
Seated them on skins of ermine,
105   And the careful old Nokomis

Brought them food in bowls of bass-wood,
Water brought in birchen dippers,
And the calumet, the peace-pipe,
Filled and lighted for their smoking.
110   All the old men of the village,
All the warriors of the nation,
All the Jossakeeds, the prophets,
The magicians, the Wabenos,
And the medicine-men, the Medas,
115   Came to bid the strangers welcome;
"It is well," they said, "O brothers,
That you come so far to see us;"
        In a circle round the doorway,
With their pipes they sat in silence,
120   Waiting to behold the strangers,
Waiting to receive their message;
Till the Black-Robe chief, the Pale-face,
From the wigwam came to greet them,
Stammering in his speech a little,
125   Speaking words yet unfamiliar;
"It is well," they said, "O brother,
That you come so far to see us!"
        Then the Black-Robe chief, the prophet,
Told his message to the people,
130   Told the purport of his mission,
Told them of the Virgin Mary,
And her blessed Son, the Saviour,
How in distant lands and ages
He had lived on earth as we do;
135   How he fasted, prayed, and labored;
How the Jews, the tribe accursed,
Mocked him, scourged him, crucified him;
How he rose from where they laid him,
Walked again with his disciples,
140   And ascended into heaven.
And the chiefs made answer, saying:
"We have listened to your message,
We have heard your words of wisdom,
We will think on what you tell us.
145   It is well for us, O brothers,
That you come so far to see us!"

Then they rose up and departed
Each one homeward to his wigwam,
To the young men and the women
150   Told the story of the strangers
Whom the Master of Life had sent them
From the shining land of Wabun.

"Then the Black-Robe chief, the prophet,
Told his message to the people."

Heavy with the heat and silence
Grew the afternoon of Summer,
155   With a drowsy sound the forest
Whispered round the sultry wigwam,
With a sound of sleep the water
Rippled on the beach below it;
From the corn-fields shrill and ceaseless
160   Sang the grasshopper, Pah-puk-keena;

And the guests of Hiawatha,
Weary with the heat of Summer,
Slumbered in the sultry wigwam.
      Slowly o'er the simmering landscape
165   Fell the evening's dusk and coolness,
And the long and level sunbeams
Shot their spears into the forest,
Breaking through its shields of shadow,
Rushed into each secret ambush,
170   Searched each thicket, dingle, hollow;
Still the guests of Hiawatha
Slumbered in the silent wigwam.
      From his place rose Hiawatha,
Bade farewell to old Nokomis,
175   Spake in whispers, spake in this wise,
Did not wake the guests, that slumbered:
      "I am going, O Nokomis,
On a long and distant journey,
To the portals of the Sunset,
180   To the regions of the home-wind,
Of the Northwest wind, Keewaydin.
But these guests I leave behind me,
In your watch and ward I leave them;
See that never harm comes near them,
185   See that never fear molests them,
Never danger nor suspicion,
Never want of food or shelter,
In the lodge of Hiawatha!"
      Forth into the village went he,
190   Bade farewell to all the warriors,
Bade farewell to all the young men,
Spake persuading, spake in this wise:
      "I am going, O my people,
On a long and distant journey;
195   Many moons and many winters
Will have come, and will have vanished,
Ere I come again to see you.
But my guests I leave behind me;
Listen to their words of wisdom,
200   Listen to the truth they tell you,
For the Master of Life has sent them

From the land of light and morning!"
On the shore stood Hiawatha,
Turned and waved his hand at parting;
205   On the clear and luminous water
Launched his birch canoe for sailing,
From the pebbles of the margin
Shoved it forth into the water;
Whispered to it, "Westward! westward!"
210   And with speed it darted forward.
And the evening sun descending
Set the clouds on fire with redness,
Burned the broad sky, like a prairie,
Left upon the level water
215   One long track and trail of splendor,
Down whose stream, as down a river,
Westward, westward Hiawatha
Sailed into the fiery sunset,
Sailed into the purple vapors,
220   Sailed into the dusk of evening.
And the people from the margin
Watched him floating, rising, sinking,
Till the birch canoe seemed lifted
High into that sea of splendor,
225   Till it sank into the vapors
Like the new moon slowly, slowly
Sinking in the purple distance.
And they said, "Farewell forever!"
Said, "Farewell, O Hiawatha!"
230   And the forests, dark and lonely,
Moved through all their depths of darkness,
Sighed, "Farewell, O Hiawatha!"
And the waves upon the margin
Rising, rippling on the pebbles,
235   Sobbed, "Farewell, O Hiawatha!"
And the heron, the Shuh-shuh-gah,
From her haunts among the fen-lands,
Screamed, "Farewell, O Hiawatha!"
Thus departed Hiawatha,
240   Hiawatha the Beloved,
In the glory of the sunset,
In the purple mists of evening,

To the regions of the home-wind,
Of the Northwest wind, Keewaydin,
245 To the Islands of the Blessed,
To the kingdom of Ponemah,
To the land of the Hereafter!

THE SKELETON IN ARMOR.

[The following Ballad was suggested to me while riding on thesea-shore at Newport. A year or two previous a skeleton had been dugup at Fall River, clad in broken and corroded armor; and the ideaoccurred to me of connecting it with the Round Tower at Newport,generally known hitherto as the Old Wind-Mill, though now claimed bythe Danes as a work of their early ancestors. Professor Rafn, in the*Mémoires de la Société Royale des Antiquaires du Nord*, for1838-1839, says:

"There is no mistaking in this instance the style in which the morean-cient stone edifices of the North were constructed, the stylewhich belongs to the Roman or Ante-Gothic architecture, and which,especially, after the time of Charlemagne, diffused itself fro-mItaly over the whole of the West and the North of Europe, where itcontinued to predominate until the close of the 12th century; thatstyle, which some authors have, from one of its most strikingchar-acteristics, called the round arch style, the same which inEngland is denominated Saxon and sometimes Norman architecture.

"On the ancient structure in Newport there are no ornamentsremaining, which might possible have served to guide us in assigningthe probably date of its erection. That no vestige whatever is foundof the pointed arch nor any approximation to it, is indicative ofan earlier rather than of a later period. From such characteristicsas remain, however, we can scarcely form any other inference thanone, in which I am persuaded that all, who are familiar withOld-Northern architecture will concur, THAT THIS BUILDING WASERECTED AT A PERIOD DECIDEDLY NOT LATER THAN THE 12TH CENTURY. Thisre-mark applies, of course, to the original building only, and not tothe alterations that it subsequently received; for there are severalsuch al-terations in the upper part of the building which cannot bemistaken, and which were most likely occasioned by its being adaptedin modern times to various uses, for example as the substructure ofa wind-mill, and latterly as a hay magazine. To the same times maybe referred the windows, the fireplace, and the apertures made abovethe columns. That this building could not have been erected for awind-mill, is what an architect will easily discern."

I will not enter into a discussion of the point. It is sufficientlywell established for the purpose of a ballad; though doubtless manyan honest citizen of Newport, who has passed his days within sightof the Round Tower, will be ready to exclaim with Sancho; "God blessme! did I not warn you to have a care of what you were doing, forthat it was nothing but a wind-mill; and nobody could mistake it,but one who had the like in his head."]

> "Speak! speak! thou fearful guest!
> Who, with thy hollow breast
> Still in rude armor drest,
>   Comest to daunt me!
> Wrapt not in Eastern balms,
> But with thy fleshless palms
> Stretched, as if asking alms,
>   Why dost thou haunt me?"
>
> Then, from those cavernous eyes
> Pale flashes seemed to rise,
> As when the Northern skies
>   Gleam in December;
> And, like the water's flow
> Under December's snow,
> Came a dull voice of woe
>   From the heart's chamber.
>
> "I was a Viking old!
> My deeds, though manifold,
> No Skald in song has told,
>   No Saga taught thee!
> Take heed, that in thy verse
> Thou dost the tale rehearse,
> Else dread a dead man's curse!
>   For this I sought thee.

178

"Far in the Northern Land,
By the wild Baltic's strand,
I, with my childish hand,
      Tamed the ger-falcon;
And, with my skates fast-bound,
Skimmed the half-frozen Sound,
That the poor whimpering hound
      Trembled to walk on.

"Oft to his frozen lair
Tracked I the grisly bear,
While from my path the hare
      Fled like a shadow;
Oft through the forest dark
Followed the were-wolf's bark
Until the soaring lark
      Sang from the meadow.

"But when I older grew,
Joining a corsair's crew,
O'er the dark sea I flew
      With the marauders.
Wild was the life we led;
Many the souls that sped,
Many the hearts that bled,
      By our stern orders.

"Many a wassail-bout
Wore the long Winter out;
Often our midnight shout
      Set the cocks crowing,
As we the Berserk's tale
Measured in cups of ale,
Draining the oaken pail,
      Filled to o'erflowing.

"Once as I told in glee
Tales of the stormy sea,
Soft eyes did gaze on me,
      Burning yet tender;
And as the white stars shine

179

On the dark Norway pine,
On that dark heart of mine
Fell their soft splendor.

"I wooed the blue-eyed maid;
Yielding, yet half afraid,
And in the forest's shade
          Our vows were plighted.
Under its loosened vest
Fluttered her little breast,
Like birds within their nest
By the hawk frighted.

"Bright in her father's hall
Shields gleamed upon the wall,
Loud sang the minstrels all,
          Chaunting his glory;
When of old Hildebrand
I asked his daughter's hand,
Mute did the minstrels stand
          To hear my story,

"While the brown ale he quaffed,
Loud then the champion laughed,
And as the wind-gusts waft
          The sea-foam brightly,
So the loud laugh of scorn,
Out of those lips unshorn,
From the deep drinking-horn
          Blew the foam lightly.

"She was a Prince's child,
I but a Viking wild,
And though she blushed and smiled,
          I was discarded!
Should not the dove so white
Follow the sea-mew's flight,
Why did they leave that night
          Her nest unguarded?

"Scarce had I put to sea,

Bearing the maid with me,—
Fairest of all was she
        Among the Norsemen!
When on the white sea-strand,
Waving his armed hand,
Saw we old Hildebrand,
        With twenty horsemen.

"Then launched they to the blast
Bent like a reed each mast,
Yet we were gaining fast,
        When the wind failed us:
And with a sudden flaw
Came round the gusty Skaw,
So that our foe we saw
        Laugh as he hailed us.

"And as to catch the gale
Round veered the flapping sail,
Death! was the helmsman's hail;
        Death without quarter!
Mid-ships with iron keel
Struck we her ribs of steel;
Down her black hulk did reel
        Through the black water

"As with his wings aslant,
Sails the fierce cormorant,
Seeking some rocky haunt,
        With his prey laden,
So toward the open main,
Beating to sea again,
Through the wild hurricane,
        Bore I the maiden.

"Three weeks we westward bore,
And when the storm was o'er,
Cloud-like we saw the shore
        Stretching to lee-ward;
There for my lady's bower
Built I the lofty tower,

Which, to this very hour,
        Stands looking sea-ward.

"There lived we many years;
Time dried the maiden's tears;
She had forgot her fears,
        She was a mother;
Death closed her mild blue eyes,
Under that tower she lies;
Ne'er shall the sun arise
        On such another!

"Still grew my bosom then,
Still as a stagnant fen!
Hateful to me were men,
        The sunlight hateful!
In the vast forest here,
Clad in my warlike gear,
Fell I upon my spear,
        O, death was grateful!

"Thus, seamed with many scars,
Bursting these prison bars,
Up to its native stars
        My soul ascended!
There from the flowing bowl
Deep drinks the warrior's soul,
Skoal! to the Northland! *Skoal!*"[1]
—Thus the tale ended.

---

[1] In Scandinavia this is the customary salutation
when drinking a health. I have slightly changed the
orthography of the word, in order to preserve the correct
pronunciation.

THE WRECK OF THE HESPERUS

It was the schooner Hesperus,
    That sailed the wintry sea;
And the skipper had taken his little daughter
    To bear him company.

Blue were her eyes as the fairy-flax,
    Her cheeks like the dawn of day,
And her bosom white as the hawthorn buds,
    That ope in the month of May.

The skipper he stood beside the helm
    With his pipe in his mouth,
And watched how the veering flaw did blow
    The smoke now West, now South.

Then up and spake an old Sailor,
    Had sailed the Spanish Main,
"I pray thee, put into yonder port,
    For I fear a hurricane.

"Last night, the moon had a golden ring,
    And to-night no moon we see!"
The skipper he blew a whiff from his pipe
    And a scornful laugh laughed he.

Colder and louder blew the wind,
    A gale from the Northeast;
The snow fell hissing in the brine,
    And the billows frothed like yeast.

Down came the storm, and smote amain,
    The vessel in its strength;
She shuddered and paused, like a frighted steed,
    Then leaped her cable's length.

"Come hither! come hither! my little daughter,
    And do not tremble so;
For I can weather the roughest gale,
    That ever wind did blow."

He wrapped her warm in his seaman's coat
    Against the stinging blast;
He cut a rope from a broken spar,
    And bound her to the mast.

"O father! I hear the church-bells ring,
    O say, what may it be?"
"'T is a fog-bell on a rock-bound coast,"
    And he steered for the open sea.

"O father! I hear the sound of guns,
    O say, what may it be?"
"Some ship in distress, that cannot live
    In such an angry sea!"

"O father! I see a gleaming light,
    O say, what may it be?"
But the father answered never a word
    A frozen corpse was he.

Lashed to the helm, all stiff and stark,
    With his face to the skies,
The lantern gleamed through the gleaming snow
    On his fixed and glassy eyes.

Then the maiden clasped her hands and prayed
    That saved she might be;
And she thought of Christ, who stilled the wave,
    On the Lake of Galilee.

And fast through the midnight dark and drear,
    Through the whistling sleet and snow,
Like a sheeted ghost, the vessel swept
    Towards the reef of Norman's Woe.

And ever the fitful gusts between
    A sound came from the land;
It was the sound of the trampling surf,
    On the rocks and the hard sea-sand.

The breakers were right beneath her bows,
    She drifted a dreary wreck,
And a whooping billow swept the crew
    Like icicles from her deck.

She struck where the white and fleecy waves
    Looked soft as carded wool,
But the cruel rocks, they gored her side
    Like the horns of an angry bull.

Her rattling shrouds, all sheathed in ice,
    With the masts went by the board;
Like a vessel of glass, she strove and sank
    Ho! Ho! the breakers roared!

At daybreak, on the bleak sea-beach,
    A fisherman stood aghast,
To see the form of a maiden fair,
    Lashed close to a drifting mast.

The salt sea was frozen on her breast
    The salt tears in her eyes;
And he saw her hair, like the brown sea weed
    On the billows fall and rise.

Such was the wreck of the Hesperus,
    In the midnight and the snow!
Christ save us all from a death like this
    On the reef of Norman's Woe!

THE LUCK OF EDENHALL.

FROM THE GERMAN OF UHLAND.

[The tradition, upon which this ballad is founded, and the "shards of the Luck of Edenhall," still exist in England. The goblet is in the possession of Sir Christopher Musgrave, Bart., of Eden Hall, Cumberland; and is not so entirely shattered, as the ballad leaves it.]

Of Edenhall, the youthful Lord
Bids sound the festal trumpet's call:
He rises at the banquet board,
And cries, 'mid the drunken revelers all,
"Now bring me the Luck of Edenhall!"

The butler hears the words with pain,
The house's oldest seneschal,
Takes slow from its silken cloth again
The drinking glass of crystal tall;
They call it the Luck of Edenhall.

Then said the Lord: "This glass to praise,
Fill with red wine from Portugal!"
The gray-beard with trembling hand obeys;
A purple light shines over all,
It beams from the Luck of Edenhall.

Then speaks the Lord, and waves it light:
"This glass of flashing crystal tall

Gave to my sires the Fountain-Sprite
She wrote in it: *If this glass doth fall,*
Farewell then, O Luck of Edenhall!

"'T was right a goblet the Fate should be
Of the joyous race of Edenhall!
Deep draughts drink we right willingly;
And willingly ring, with merry call,
Kling! klang! to the Luck of Edenhall!"

First rings it deep, and full, and mild,
Like to the song of a nightingale;
Then like the roar of a torrent wild;
Then mutters at last like the thunder's fall,
The glorious Luck of Edenhall.

"For its keeper takes a race of might,
The fragile goblet of crystal tall;
It has lasted longer than is right;
Kling! klang!—with a harder blow than all
Will I try the Luck of Edenhall!"

As the goblet ringing flies apart,
Suddenly cracks the vaulted hall;
And through the rift, the wild flames start;
The guests in dust are scattered all,
With the breaking Luck of Edenhall.

In storms the foe, with fire and sword;
He in the night had scaled the wall,
Slain by the sword lies the youthful Lord,
But holds in his hand the crystal tall,
The shattered Luck of Edenhall.

On the morrow the butler gropes alone,
The gray-bird in the desert hall,
He seeks his Lord's burnt skeleton,
He seeks in the dismal ruin's fall
The shards of the Luck of Edenhall.

"The stone wall," saith he, "doth fall aside,

Down must the stately columns fall;
Glass is this earth's Luck and Pride;
In athoms shall fall this earthly ball
One day like the Luck of Edenhall!"

THE ELECTED KNIGHT.

FROM THE DANISH.

[The following strange and somewhat mystical ballad
is from Nyerup and Rahbek's *Danske Viser* of the Middle
Ages. It seems to refer to the first preaching of Christiani-
ty in the North, and to the institution of Knight-Errantry.
The three maidens I suppose to be Faith, Hope, and
Charity. The irregularities of the original have been care-
fully preserved in the translation.]

Sir Oluf he rideth over the plain,
  Full seven miles broad and seven miles wide,
But never, ah never can meet with the man
  A tilt with him dare ride.

He saw under the hill-side
  A Knight full well equipped;
His steed was black, his helm was barred;
  He was riding at full speed.

He wore upon his spurs
  Twelve little golden birds;
Anon he spurred his steed with a clang,
  And there sat all the birds and sang.

He wore upon his mail
  Twelve little golden wheels;
Anon in eddies the wild wind blew,

THE ELECTED KNIGHT.

And round and round the wheels they flew.

He wore before his breast
    A lance that was poised in rest,
And it was sharper than diamond stone,
    It made Sir Oluf's heart to groan.

He wore upon his helm
    A wreath of ruddy gold;
And that gave him the Maidens Three,
    The youngest was fair to behold.

Sir Oluf questioned the Knight eftsoon
    If he were come from heaven down;
"Art thou Christ of Heaven," quoth he;
    "So will I yield me unto thee."

"I am not Christ the Great,
    Thou shallt not yield thee yet;
I am an Unknown Knight,
    Three modest Maidens have me bedight."

"Art thou a Knight elected,
    And have three Maidens thee bedight;
So shalt thou ride a tilt this day,
    For all the maidens' honor!"

The first tilt they together rode,
    They put their steeds to the test;
The second tilt they together rode,
    They proved their manhood best.

The third tilt they together rode,
    Neither of them would yield;
The fourth tilt they together rode,
The both fell on the field.

Now lie the lords upon the plains,
    And their blood runs unto death;
Now sit the Maidens in the high tower,
    The youngest sorrows till death.

THE CHILDREN OF THE LORD'S SUPPER.

FROM THE SWEDISH OF BISHOP TEGNOR

Pentecost, day of rejoicing, had come. The church of the village
Stood gleaming white in the morning's sheen. On the spire of the bel-
fry,
Tipped with a vane of metal, the friendly frames of the Spring-sun
Glanced like the tongues of fire, beheld by Apostles aforetime.
Clear was the heaven and blue, and May, with her cap crowned with
roses,
Stood in her holiday dress in the fields, and the wind and the brooklet
Murmured gladness and peace, God's-peace! With lips rosy-tinted
Whispered the race of the flowers, and merry on balancing branches
Birds were singing their carol, a jubilant hymn to the Highest.
Swept and clean was the churchyard. Adorned like a leaf-woven arbor
Stood its old-fashioned gate; and within upon each cross of iron
Hung was a sweet-scented garland, new twined by the hands of affec-
tion.
Even the dial, that stood on a fountain among the departed
(There full a hundred years had it stood), was embellished with blos-
soms.
Like to the patriarch hoary, the sage of his kith and the hamlet,
Who on his birthday is crowned by children and children's children,
So stood the ancient prophet, and mute with pencil of iron
Marked on the table of stone, and measured the swift-changing mo-
ment,
While all around at his feet, an eternity slumbered in quiet.
Also the church within was adorned, for this was the season
In which the young, their parent's hope, and the loved-ones of heaven,

Should at the foot of the altar renew the vows of their baptism.
Therefore each nook and corner was swept and cleaned, and the dust
    was
Blown from the walls and ceiling, and from the oil-painted benches.
There stood the church like a garden; the Feast of the Leafy Pavilions[1]
Saw we in living presentment. From noble arms on the church wall
Grew forth a cluster of leaves, and the preacher's pulpit of oakwood
Budded once more anew, as aforetime the rod before Aaron.
Wreathed thereon was the Bible with leaves, and the dove, washed
    with silver,
Under its conopy fastened, a necklace had on of wind-flowers.
But in front of the choir, round the altarpiece painted by Horberg,[2]
Crept a garland gigantic; and bright-curling tresses of angels
Peeped, like the sun from a cloud, out of the shadowy leaf-work.
Likewise the lustre of brass, new-polished, blinked from the ceiling,
And for lights there were lilies of Pentecost set in the sockets.
Loud rang the bells already; the thronging crowd was assembled
Far from valleys and hills, to list to the holy preaching.
Hark! then roll forth at once the mighty tones from the organ,
Hover like voices from God, aloft like invisible spirits.
Like as Elias in heaven, when he cast off from him his mantle,
Even so cast off the soul its garments of earth; and with one voice
Chimed in the congregation, and sang an anthem immortal
Of the sublime Wallin,[3] of David's harp in the North-land
Tuned to the choral of Luther; the song on its powerful pinions
Took every living soul, and lifted it gently to heaven.
And every face did shine like the Holy One's face upon Tabor.
Lo! there entered then into the church the Reverend Teacher.
Father he hight and he was in the parish; a christianly plainness
Clothed from his head to his feet the old man of seventy winters.
Friendly was he to behold, and glad as the heralding angel
Walked he among the crowds, but still a contemplative grandeur

---

[1] The Feast of the Tabernacles; in Swedish
Löfkyddohögtiden, the Leaf-huts'-high-tide.
[2] The peasant-painter of Sweden. He is known
chiefly by his altar-pieces in the village churches.
[3] A distinguished pulpit-orator and poet. He is
particularly remarkable for the beauty and sublimity of his
psalms.

Lay on his forehead as clear, as on a moss-covered grave-stone a sun-
      beam.
As in his inspiration (an evening twilight that faintly
Gleams in the human soul, even now, from the day of creation)
Th' Artist, the friend of heaven, imagines Saint John when in Pat-
      mos;—
Gray, with his eyes uplifted to heaven, so seemed then the old man;
Such was the glance of his eye, and such were his tresses of silver.
All the congregation arose in the pews that were numbered,
But with a cordial look, to the right and the left hand, the old man
Nodding all hail and peace, disappeared in the innermost chancel.

Simply and solemnly now proceeded the Christian service,
Singing and prayer, and at last an ardent discourse from the old man.
Many a moving word and warning, that out of the heart came
Fell like the dew of the morning, like manna on those in the desert.
Afterwards, when all was finished, the Teacher reentered the chancel,
Followed therein by the young. On the right hand the boys had their
      places
Delicate figures, with close-curling hair and cheeks rosy-blooming.
But on the left-hand of these, there stood the tremulous lilies,
Tinged with the blushing light of the morning, the diffident maid-
      ens,—
Folding their hands in prayer, and their eyes cast down on the pave-
      ment.
Now came, with question and answer, the catechism. In the beginning
Answered the children with troubled and faltering voice, but the old
      man's
Glances of kindness encouraged them soon, and the doctrines eternal
Flowed, like the waters of fountains, so clear from lips unpolluted.
Whene'er the answer was closed, and as oft as they named the Re-
      deemer,
Lowly louted the boys, and lowly the maidens all courtesied.
Friendly the Teacher stood, like an angel of light there among them,
And to the children explained he the holy, the highest, in few words,
Thorough, yet simple and clear, for sublimity always is simple,
Both in sermon and song a child can seize on its meaning.
Even as the green-growing bud is unfolded when Spring-tide ap-
      proaches
Leaf by leaf is developed, and, warmed by the radiant sunshine,
Blushes with purple and gold, till at last the perfected blossom

Opens its odorous chalice, and rocks with its crown in the breezes,
So was unfolded here the Christian lore of salvation,
Line by line from the soul of childhood. The fathers and mothers
Stood behind them in tears, and were glad at each well-worded an-
    swer.

Now went the old man up to the altar;—and straightway transfigured
(So did it seem unto me) was then the affectionate Teacher,
Like the Lord's Prophet sublime, and awful as Death and as Judgment
Stood he, the God-commissioned, the soul-searcher, earthward de-
    scending,
Glances, sharp as a sword, into hearts, that to him were transparent
Shot he; his voice was deep, was low like the thunder afar off.
So on a sudden transfigured he stood there, he spake and he ques-
    tioned.

"This is the faith of the Fathers, the faith the Apostles delivered,
This is moreover the faith whereunto I baptized you, while still ye
Lay on your mothers' breasts, and nearer the portals of heaven.
Slumbering received you then the Holy Church in its bosom;
Wakened from sleep are ye now, and the light in the radiant splendor
Rains from the heaven downward;—to-day on the threshhold of child-
    hood
Kindly she frees you again, to examine and make your election,
For she knows nought of compulsion, only conviction desireth.
This is the hour of your trial, the turning-point of existence,
Seed for the coming days; without revocation departeth
Now from your lips the confession; Bethink ye, before ye make an-
    swer!
Think not! O think not with guile to deceive the questioning Teacher.
Sharp is his eye to-day, and a curse ever rests upon falsehood.
Enter not with a lie on Life's journey; the multitude hears you,
Brothers and sisters and parents, what dear upon earth is and holy
Standeth before your sight as a witness; the Judge everlasting
Looks from the sun down upon you, and angels in waiting beside him
Grave your confession in letters of fire, upon tablets eternal.
Thus then,—believe ye in God, in the Father who this world created?
Him who redeemed it, the Son, and the Spirit where both are united?
Will ye promise me here (a holy promise), to cherish
God more than all things earthly, and every man as a brother?
Will ye promise me here, to confirm your faith by your living,

Th' heavenly faith of affection! to hope, to forgive, and to suffer,
Be what it may your condition, and walk before God in uprightness?
Will ye promise me this before God and man?'—With a clear voice
Answered the young men Yes! and Yes! with lips softly-breathing
Answered the maidens eke. Then dissolved from the brow of the
    Teacher
Clouds with the thunders therein, and he spake on in accents more
    gentle,
Soft as the evening's breath, as harps by Babylon's rivers.

"Hail, then, hail to you all! To the heirdom of heaven be ye welcome!
Children no more from this day, but by covenant brothers and sisters!
Yet,—for what reason not children? Of such is the kingdom of heaven.
Here upon earth an assemblage of children, in heaven one father,
Ruling them as his own household,—forgiving in turn and chastising,
That is of human life a picture, as Scripture has taught us.
Blessed are the pure before God! Upon purity and upon virtue
Resteth the Christian Faith; she herself from on high is descended.
Strong as a man and pure as a child, is the sum of the doctrine,
Which the Godlike delivered, and on the cross suffered and died for.
O! as ye wander this day from childhood's sacred asylum
Downward and ever downward, and deeper in Age's chill valley,
O! how soon will ye come,—too soon!—and long to turn backward
Up to its hill-tops again, to the sun-illumined, where Judgment
Stood like a father before you, and Pardon, clad like a mother,
Gave you her hand to kiss, and the loving heart was forgiven,
Life was a play and your hands grasped after the roses of heaven!
Seventy years have I lived already; the Father eternal
Gave to me gladness and care; but the loveliest hours of existence,
When I have steadfastly gazed in their eyes, I have instantly known
    them,
Known them all, all again;—they were my childhood's acquaintance.
Therefore take from henceforth, as guides in the paths of existence,
Prayer, with her eyes raised to heaven, and Innocence, bride of man's
    childhood.
Innocence, child beloved, is a guest from the world of the blessed.
Beautiful, and in her hand a lily; on life's roaring billows
Swings she in safety, she heeded them not, in the ship she was sleep-
    ing.
Calmly she gazes around in the turmoil of men; in the desert
Angels descend and minister unto her; she herself knoweth

Naught of her glorious attendance; but follows faithful and humble,
Follows so long as she may her friend; O do not reject her,
For she cometh from God and she holdeth the keys of the heavens.—
Prayer is Innocence' friend; and willingly flieth incessant
'Twixt the earth and the sky, the carrier-pigeon of heaven.
Son of Eternity, fettered in Time, and an exile, the Spirit
Tugs at his chains evermore, and struggles like flames ever upward.
Still he recalls with emotion his father's manifold mansions.
Thinks of the land of his fathers, where blossomed more freshly the
        flowers,
Shone a more beautiful sun, and he played with the winged angels.
Then grows the earth too narrow, too close; and homesick for heaven
Longs the wanderer again; and the Spirit's longings are worship;
Worship is called his most beautiful hour, and its tongue is entreaty.
Ah! when the infinite burden of life descendeth upon us,
Crushes to earth our hope, and, under the earth, in the grave-yard,
Then it is good to pray unto God; for his sorrowing children
Turns he ne'er from his door, but he heals and helps and consoles
        them.
Yet it is better to pray when all things are prosperous with us,
Pray in fortunate days, for life's most beautiful Fortune
Kneels down before the Eternal's throne; and, with hands interfolded,
Praises thankful and moved the only Giver of blessings.
Or do ye know, ye children, one blessing that comes not from Heaven?
What has mankind forsooth, the poor! that it has not received?
Therefore, fall in the dust and pray! The seraphs adoring
Cover with pinions six their face in the glory of him who
Hung his masonry pendant on naught, when the world he created.
Earth declareth his might, and the firmament uttereth his glory.
Races blossom and die, and stars fall downward from heaven,
Downward like withered leaves: at the last stroke of midnight, millen-
        niums
Lay themselves down at his feet, and he sees them, but counts them as
        nothing.
Who shall stand in his presence? The wrath of the Judge is terrific,
Casting the insolent down at a glance. When he speaks in his anger
Hillocks skip like the kid, and the mountains leap like the roe-buck.
Yet,—why are ye afraid, ye children? This awful avenger,
Ah! is a merciful God! God's voice was not in the earthquake,
Not in the fire, nor the storm, but it was in the whispering breezes.
Love is the root of creation; God's essence; worlds without number

202

Lie in his bosom like children; he made them for this purpose only.
Only to love and to be loved again, he breathed forth his spirit
Into the slumbering dust, and upright standing, it laid its
Hand on its heart, and felt it was warm with a flame out of heaven.
Quench, O quench not that flame! It is the breath of your being.
Love is life, but hatred is death. Not father nor mother
Loved you, as God has loved you; for it was that you may be happy
Gave he his only son. When he bowed down his head in the death-
hour
Solemnized Love its triumph; the sacrifice then was completed.
Lo! then was rent on a sudden the vail of the temple, dividing
Earth and heaven apart, and the dead from their sepulchers rising
Whispered with pallid lips and low in the ears of each other
Th' answer, but dreamed of before, to creation's enigma,—Atonement!
Depths of Love are Atonement's depths, for Love is Atonement.
Therefore, child of mortality, love thou the merciful Father;
Wish what the Holy One wishes, and not from fear, but affection;
Fear is the virtue of slaves; but the heart that loveth is willing;
Perfect was before God, and perfect is Love, and Love only.
Lovest thou God as thou oughtest, then lovest thou likewise thy breth-
ren;
One is the sun in Heaven, and one, only one is love also.
Bears not each human figure the godlike stamp on his forehead?
Readest thou not in his face thine origin? Is he not sailing
Lost like thyself on an ocean unknown, and is he not guided
By the same stars that guide thee? Why shouldst thou hate then thy
brother?
Hateth he thee, forgive! For 'tis sweet to stammer one letter
Of the Eternal's language;—on earth it is called Forgiveness!
Knowest thou Him, who forgave, with the crown of thorns round his
temples?
Earnestly prayed for his foes, for his murderers? Say, dost thou know
him?
Ah! thou confessest his name, so follow likewise his example,
Think of thy brother no ill, but throw a vail over his failings,
Guide the erring aright; for the good, the heavenly shepherd
Took the lost lamb in his arms, and bore it back to its mother.
This is the fruit of Love, and it is by its fruits that we know it.
Love is the creature's welfare, with God; but Love among mortals
Is but an endless sigh! He longs, and endures, and stands waiting,
Suffers and yet rejoices, and smiles with tears on his eyelids.

Hope,—so is called upon earth, his recompense.—Hope, the befriend-
    ing,
Does what she can, for she points evermore up to heaven, and faithful
Plunges her anchor's peak in the depths of the grave, and beneath it
Paints a more beautiful world, a dim, but a sweet play of shadows!
Races, better than we, have leaned on her wavering promise,
Having naught else beside Hope. Then praise we our Father in Heav-
    en,
Him, who has given us more; for to us has Hope been illumined,
Groping no longer in night; she is Faith, she is living assurance.
Faith is enlightened Hope; she is light, is the eye of affection
Dreams of the longing interprets, and carves their visions in marble.
Faith is the sun of life; and her countenance shines like the Prophet's,
For she has looked upon God; the heaven on its stable foundation
Draws she with chains down to earth, and the New Jerusalem sinketh
Splendid with portals twelve in golden vapors descending.
There enraptured she wanders, and looks at the figures majestic,
Fears not the winged crowd, in the midst of them all is her homestead.
Therefore love and believe; for works will follow spontaneous
Even as day does the sun; the Right from the Good is an offspring,
Love in a bodily shape; and Christian works are no more than
Animate Love and faith, as flowers are the animate spring-tide.
Works do follow us all unto God; there stand and bear witness
Not what they seemed,—but what they were only. Blessed is he who
Hears their confession secure; they are mute upon earth until death's
    hand
Opens the mouth of the silent. Ye children does Death e'er alarm you?
Death is the brother of Love, twin-brother is he, and is only
More austere to behold. With a kiss upon lips that are fading
Takes he the soul and departs, and rocked in arms of affection,
Places the ransomed child, new born, 'fore the face of its father.
Sounds of his coming already I hear,—see dimly his pinions,
Swart as the night, but with stars strewn upon them! I fear not before
    him.
Death is only release, and in mercy is mute. On his bosom
Freer breathes, in its coolness, my breast; and face to face standing
Look I on God as he is, a sun unpolluted by vapors;
Look on the light of the ages I loved, the spirits majestic,
Nobler, better than I; they stand by the throne all transfigured,
Vested in white, and with harps of gold, and are singing an anthem,
Writ in the climate of heaven, in the language spoken by angels.

You, in like manner, ye children beloved, he one day shall gather,
Never forgets he the weary;—then welcome, ye loved ones, hereafter!
Meanwhile forget not the keeping of vows, forget not the promise,
Wander from holiness onward to holiness; earth shall ye heed not;
Earth is but dust and heaven is light; I have pledged you to heaven.
God of the Universe, hear me! thou fountain of Love everlasting,
Hark to the voice of thy servant! I send up my prayer to thy heaven!
Let me hereafter not miss at thy throne one spirit of all these,
Whom thou hast given me here! I have loved them all like a father.
May they bear witness for me, that I taught them the way of salvation,
Faithful, so far as I knew of thy word: again may they know me,
Fall on their Teacher's breast, and before thy face may I place them,
Pure as they now are, but only more tried, and exclaiming with glad-
        ness,
Father, lo! I am here, and the children, whom thou hast given me!"

Weeping he spake in these words; and now at the beck of the old man
Knee against knee they knitted a wreath round the altar's enclosure.
Kneeling he read then the prayers of the consecration, and softly
With him the children read; at the close, with tremulous accents,
Asked he the peace of heaven, a benediction upon them.
Now should have ended his task for the day; the following Sunday
Was for the young appointed to eat of the Lord's holy Supper.
Sudden, as struck from the clouds, stood the Teacher silent and laid his
Hand on his forehead, and cast his looks upward; while thoughts high
        and holy
Flew through the midst of his soul, and his eyes glanced with wonder-
        ful brightness.
"On the next Sunday, who knows! perhaps I shall rest in the grave-
        yard!
Some one perhaps of yourselves, a lily broken untimely,
Bow down his head to the earth; why delay I? the hour is accom-
        plished.
Warm is the heart;—I will so! for to-day grows the harvest of heaven.
What I began accomplish I now; for what failing therein is
I, the old man, will answer to God and the reverend father.
Say to me only, ye children, ye denizens new-come in heaven,
Are ye ready this day to eat of the bread of Atonement?
What it denoteth, that know ye full well, I have told it you often.
Of the new covenant a symbol it is, of Atonement a token,

'Stablished between earth and heaven. Man by his sins and transgres-
     sions
Far has wandered from God, from his essence. 'Twas in the beginning
Fast by the Tree of Knowledge he fell, and it hangs its crown o'er the
Fall to this day; in the Thought is the Fall; in the Heart the Atonement.
Infinite is the Fall, the Atonement infinite likewise.
See! behind me, as far as the old man remembers, and forward,
Far as Hope in her flight can reach with her wearied pinions,
Sin and Atonement incessant go through the lifetime of mortals.
Brought forth is sin full-grown; but Atonement sleeps in our bosoms
Still as the cradled babe; and dreams of heaven and of angels
Cannot wake to sensation; is like the tones in the harp's strings,
Spirits imprisoned, that wait evermore the deliverer's finger.
Therefore, ye children beloved, descended the Prince of Atonement,
Woke the slumberer from sleep, and he stands now with eyes all re-
     splendent,
Bright as the vault of the sky, and battles with Sin and o'ercomes her
Downward to earth he came and transfigured thence reascended,
Not from the heart in likewise, for there he still lives in the Spirit,
Loves and atones evermore. So long as Time is, is Atonement.
Therefore with reverence receive this day her visible token.
Tokens are dead if the things do not live. The light everlasting
Unto the blind man is not, but is born of the eye that has vision.
Neither in bread nor in wine, but in the heart that is hallowed
Lieth forgivenes enshrined; the intention alone of amendment.
Fruits of the earth ennobles to heavenly things, and removes all
Sin and the guerdon of sin. Only Love with his arms wide extended,
Penitence weeping and praying; the Will that is tried, and whose gold
     flows
Purified forth from the flames; in a word, mankind by Atonement
Breaketh Atonement's bread, and drinketh Atonement's wine cup.
But he who cometh up hither, unworthy with hate in his bosom.
Scoffing at men and at God, is guilty of Christ's blessed body,
And the Redeemer's blood! To himself he eateth and drinketh
Death and doom! And from this, preserve us, thou heavenly Father!
Are ye ready, ye children, to eat of the bread of Atonement?"
Thus with emotion he asked, and together answered the children
Yes! with deep sobs interrupted. Then read he the due supplications,
Read the Form of Communion, and in chimed the organ and anthem;
O! Holy Lamb of God, who takest away our transgressions.
Hear us! give us thy peace! have mercy, have mercy upon us!

Th' old man, with trembling hand, and heavenly pearls on his eyelids,
Filled now the chalice and paten, and dealt round the mystical sym-
    bols.
O! then seemed it to me, as if God, with the broad eye of mid-day,
Clearer looked in at the windows, and all the trees in the churchyard
Bowed down their summits of green and the grass on the graves 'gan
    to shiver.
But in the children (I noted it well; I knew it) there ran a
Tremor of holy rapture along through their ice-cold members.
Decked like an altar before them, there stood the green earth, and
    above it
Heaven opened itself, as of old before Stephen; there saw they
Radiant in glory the Father, and on his right hand the Redeemer.
Under them hear they the clang of harp-strings, and angels from gold
    clouds
Beckon to them like brothers, and fan with their pinions of purple.
Closed was the Teacher's task, and with heaven in their hearts and
    their faces,
Up rose the children all, and each bowed him, weeping full sorely,
Downward to kiss that reverend hand, but all of them pressed he
Moved to his bosom, and laid, with a prayer, his hands full of bless-
    ings,
Now on the holy breast, and now on the innocent tresses.

The Adventures of Sajo and her Beaver People
Grey Owl
Benediction Classics, 2011
164 pages
ISBN: 978-1849024655

Available from
www.amazon.com,
www.amazon.co.uk

Grey Owl's children's story,
first published in 1935. This
delightful novel comes com-
plete with Grey Owl's original
drawings, chapter head-pieces
and a glossary of Ojibway Indian words.

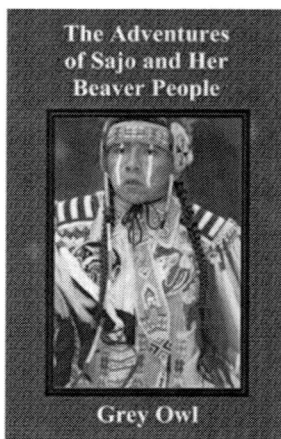

Laxdæla Saga -
The Laxdale Saga
Benediction Classics, 2011
204 pages
ISBN: 978-1-84902-431-0
Available from www.amazon.com,
www.amazon.co.uk

Laxdaela saga is a 13th century Icelandic
saga, telling the story of the people in the
Breiðafjörður area from the late 9th cen-
tury to the early 11th century. The saga
tells of a love triangle between Guðrún Ósvífrsdóttir, Kjartan Ólafsson
and Bolli Þorleiksson. Kjartan and Bolli are two lads who are close
friends but they both love Guðrún which causes hatred between them
and results in tragedy. Numerous ancient manuscripts contain this sa-
ga, dating back to the fourteenth century and it is second only to the
Njáls saga in the number of medieval manuscripts preserved. Laxdœla
saga is a popular story because of its poetic beauty and pathetic senti-
ment. This version contains an illustration and the original marginal
sub-headings interweaved in the text.

American History Stories
Volumes I-IV
Mara L. Pratt
Benediction Classics,2011
Each c200 pages
ISBN:
Vol I   978-1-84902-412-9
Vol II   978-1-84902-410-5
Vol III 978-1-84902-409-9
Vol IV 978-1-84902-407-5

Available from www.amazon.com,
www.amazon.co.uk

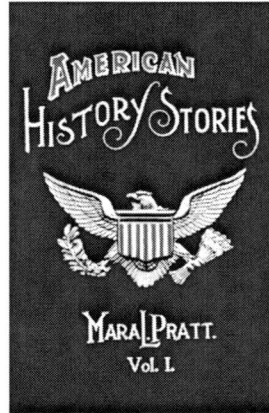

History is brought to life in these four volumes of Mara L. Pratt's re-telling of the history of America, first published in 1891. The recommended reading age is 8-12, and the chapters are short with black and white illustrations, providing a wonderful introduction for children to American history. They are so compelling that adults will enjoy them as much as the children.

The first volume begins with the story from Long Ago and ends with how the colonies great together.

The second volume tells tales of the Revolutionary times, including the reasons for the American Revolution, the courage of those defending liberty, the early battles and the heroes who led the colonists to victory.

The third volume covers the period from the end or the Revolutionary War to the middle of the 19th Century. The chapters cover the Washington and Jefferson administrations, the War of 1812 and some Indian Wars, as well as a series of fascinating well-known characters of the period.

The final volume covers the period of great conflict from Lincoln becoming president and the southern states seceding until the end of the civil war.

Also from Benediction Books ...
Wandering Between Two Worlds: Essays on Faith and Art
Anita Mathias
Benediction Books, 2007
152 pages
ISBN: 0955373700

Available from www.amazon.com, www.amazon.co.uk

In these wide-ranging lyrical essays, Anita Mathias writes, in lush, lovely prose, of her naughty Catholic childhood in Jamshedpur, India; her large, eccentric family in Mangalore, a sea-coast town converted by the Portuguese in the sixteenth century; her rebellion and atheism as a teenager in her Himalayan boarding school, run by German missionary nuns, St. Mary's Convent, Nainital; and her abrupt religious conversion after which she entered Mother Teresa's convent in Calcutta as a novice. Later rich, elegant essays explore the dualities of her life as a writer, mother, and Christian in the United States-- Domesticity and Art, Writing and Prayer, and the experience of being "an alien and stranger" as an immigrant in America, sensing the need for roots.

About the Author

Anita Mathias is the author of *Wandering Between Two Worlds: Essays on Faith and Art*. She has a B.A. and M.A. in English from Somerville College, Oxford University, and an M.A. in Creative Writing from the Ohio State University, USA. Anita won a National Endowment of the Arts fellowship in Creative Nonfiction in 1997. She lives in Oxford, England with her husband, Roy, and her daughters, Zoe and Irene.

Anita's website:
    http://www.anitamathias.com, and
Anita's blog Dreaming Beneath the Spires:
    http://dreamingbeneaththespires.blogspot.com

The Church That Had Too Much
Anita Mathias
Benediction Books, 2010
52 pages
ISBN: 9781849026567

Available from www.amazon.com, www.amazon.co.uk

The Church That Had Too Much was very well-intentioned. She
wanted to love God, she wanted to love people, but she was both ham-
pered by her muchness and the abundance of her possessions, and
beset by ambition, power struggles and snobbery. Read about the sur-
prising way The Church That Had Too Much began to resolve her
problems in this deceptively simple and enchanting fable.

About the Author

Anita Mathias is the author of *Wandering Between Two Worlds: Es-
says on Faith and Art.* She has a B.A. and M.A. in English from
Somerville College, Oxford University, and an M.A. in Creative Writ-
ing from the Ohio State University, USA. Anita won a National
Endowment of the Arts fellowship in Creative Nonfiction in 1997.
She lives in Oxford, England with her husband, Roy, and her daugh-
ters, Zoe and Irene.

Anita's website:
    http://www.anitamathias.com, and
Anita's blog Dreaming Beneath the Spires:
    http://dreamingbeneaththespires.blogspot.com

CPSIA information can be obtained at www.ICGtesting.com
Printed in the USA
BVOW07*1100211014

371687BV00015B/492/P